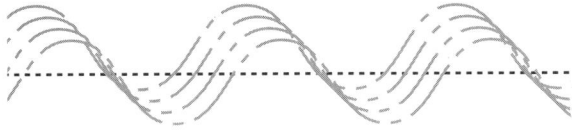

The Waite Group®

Sound Effects Playhouse

CREATE, EXPLORE, AND MANIPULATE SOUND ON YOUR PC

Kevin Weiner

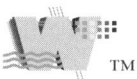

WAITE GROUP
PRESS™

Publisher · *Mitchell Waite*
Editorial Director· *Scott Calamar*
Managing Editor · *Joel Fugazzotto*
Content Editor · *Heidi Brumbaugh*
Technical Reviewer · *Gary Maddox*
Production Director · *Julianne Ososke*
Cover Design · *Michael Rogondino*
Illustrations · *Pamela Drury-Wattenmaker*
Design · *Cecile Kaufman*
Production · *LeeAnn Nelson*
Chapter Opener Art · *Tim Forcade. Tim Forcade's photographs were produced using sound synthesizing and processing systems of his own design. These images may actually be heard. Tim is an artist, designer, and a regular contributor to computer graphic publications on subjects including 3-D graphics and animation. His work has been exhibited in the United States, Canada, Europe, and Japan.*

Library of Congress Cataloging-in-Publication Data
Weiner, Kevin.
    Sound effects playhouse : create, explore, and manipulate sound on your PC / Kevin Weiner.
        p.   cm.
        Includes index.
        ISBN 1-878739-36-0 : $24.95
        1. Microcomputers.   2. Computer sound processing.   I. Title.
QA76.5.W453 1993   93-5683
006.5--dc20   CIP

TABLE OF CONTENTS

CONTENTS

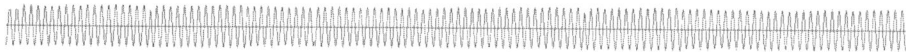

DEDICATION

to my parents, Helen and Richard

Dear Reader:

What is a book? Is it perpetually fated to be inky words on a paper page? Or can a book simply be something that inspires—feeding your head with ideas and creativity regardless of the medium? The latter, I believe. That's why I'm always pushing our books to a higher plane; using new technology to reinvent the medium.

I wrote my first book in 1973, *Projects in Sights, Sounds, and Sensations.* I like to think of it as our first multimedia book. In the years since then, I've learned that people want to *experience* information, not just passively absorb it—they want interactive MTV in a book. With this in mind, I started my own publishing company and published **Master C,** a book/disk package that turned the PC into a C language instructor. Then we branched out to computer graphics with **Fractal Creations,** which included a color poster, 3-D glasses, and a totally rad fractal generator. Ever since, we've included disks and other goodies with most of our books. **Virtual Reality Creations** is bundled with 3-D Fresnel viewing goggles and **Walkthroughs & Flybys** comes with a multimedia CD-ROM. We've made complex multimedia accessible for any PC user with **Ray Tracing Creations, Multimedia Creations, Making Movies on Your PC, Image Lab,** and three books on Fractals.

The Waite Group continues to publish innovative multimedia books on cutting-edge topics, and of course the programming books that make up our heritage. Being a programmer myself, I appreciate clear guidance through a tricky OS, so our books come bundled with disks and CDs loaded with code, utilities, and custom controls.

By 1993, The Waite Group will have published 135 books. Our next step is to develop a new type of book, an interactive, multimedia experience involving the reader on many levels.

With this new book, you'll be trained by a computer-based instructor with infinite patience, run a simulation to visualize the topic, play a game that shows you different aspects of the subject, interact with others on-line, and have instant access to a large database on the subject. For traditionalists, there will be a full-color, paper-based book.

In the meantime, they've wired the White House for hi-tech; the information super highway has been proposed; and computers, communication, entertainment, and information are becoming inseparable. To travel in this Digital Age you'll need guidebooks. The Waite Group offers such guidance for the most important software—your mind.

We hope you enjoy this book. For a color catalog, just fill out and send in the Reader Report Card at the back of the book. You can reach me on CIS as 75146,3515, MCI mail as mwaite, and usenet as mitch@well.sf.ca.us.

Sincerely,

Mitchell Waite

Mitchell Waite
Publisher

ACKNOWLEDGMENTS

We wish to thank the following individuals who kindly contributed their time, technical assistance, and permission to use the materials upon which much of this book is based.

Gary Maddox for Blaster Master
Jamie O'Connell for SBTimbre
Craig Walsh for MicFFT
Otto Chrons and Jussi Lahdenniemi for DMP and PMP
Lance Norskog for SOX
David Gallagher and the folks at QSound for providing QSound assistance
Gordon Wanner of Starlite Software for Steven Schauer's Whoop It Up! and
    Keith Boone's Wave Editor
Bob Adams and Brantley Kelly of Command Corp. for use of the IN3 demo
Jim Young for his original songs in mod format
Larry Roberts for access to his collection of traditional American songs
Mark Koenig of Sound Source Unlimited for processed 3-D sound clips

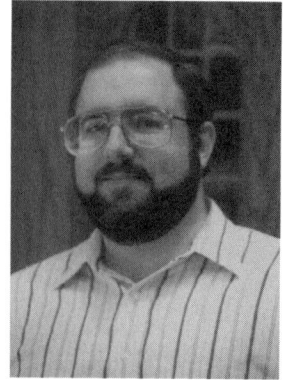

ABOUT THE AUTHOR

Kevin Weiner has spent more than half his life wrangling computers ("ornery critters," as he likes to refer to them). Fortunately, the recent trends in multimedia computing give rise to a whole new experience that he feels more than makes up for their crankiness. An avid musician whose favorite instruments are the guitar and mandolin, he is thrilled to be able to combine computing technology, which is what he knows best, with music, the thing he'd rather be doing if he were good enough to make a living at it.

Born in Bethlehem, Pennsylvania, where he still lives and works, Mr. Weiner graduated from Lehigh University in 1978 with a degree in math and information science. In an early brush with the publishing industry, he spent the next few years developing software systems at the American Newspaper Publishers Association Research Institute. Returning to Lehigh, he worked for several years in the Computing Center as a consultant, specializing in database and graphics systems. Since 1986, he has been in charge of the University's Systems Programming group, which is responsible for the deployment and support of mainframes, workstations, and PCs, along with general networking and information technologies.

In his other life, Mr. Weiner first began tinkering with computers and synthesizers in the early 1980s, just for fun. This hobby developed into a side business in which he does consulting and development of MIDI music tools and applications. Having produced a number of shareware and commercial packages, most recently a couple of products for Turtle Beach Systems, he continues to look for ways to make sound and music applications more effective and easier to use. He can be reached on CompuServe at 72416,2465.

PREFACE

Hearing is believing...

Earth has been invaded. You're in charge of defense for your sector. You survey your monitor intently, watching for signs of marauding Martians. From your right, you suddenly hear the great roar of an alien death ray. You turn to look just as it vaporizes one of your artillery batteries. A damage report crackles from the console in front of you. You shout a few commands into your microphone and then glance upward when you hear the sound of your own missiles rushing by overhead. With great anticipation, you follow them on their way to the target...a floor lamp? Snapping back to reality for a moment, you realize that you're only playing a computer game. Martians haven't landed, and you feel a little silly for turning to look in the first place.

Saving the world from disagreeable extraterrestrials is nothing new in computer games. But controlling the action with voice commands and hearing realistic sounds coming at you from all directions would have been part of science fiction just a few years ago. In this case, the game is fiction, but the technology isn't. Today, we're in the middle of a sensory revolution, and sound is at its forefront. Whatever your reasons for buying a sound card—games, music, education, presentations, or just to avoid being the only kid on the block who doesn't have one—you'll find in these pages a wealth of tools, tricks, toys, experiments, and other diversions sure to amaze, delight, and inform. Everything you need to start putting your sound card to work for you

is right here. Join the revolution today and find out for yourself why everyone's talking—including the machines.

Sound can be an exciting and fascinating subject. If you're a musician, you probably need no convincing; but if you're skeptical, we hope to change that opinion. Sound can soothe, it can evoke horror, it can bring back fond memories, it can warn of danger, and it can be a most powerful tool for communicating. Sound is something we use in many ways without even thinking about it. In this book, we'll be examining sound, and seeing much more than you may have ever thought was there. We'll slice and carve and flip and generally put it through the mill so that after it goes 'round and 'round and comes out here...well, you'll see for yourself.

Since the computer sound craze began, people have been cooking up all sorts of ways to put sounds to use in their daily activities. We'll be looking at quite a few of these applications—everything from music to sonic illusions. The aim of the Playhouse series is to let you explore the latest in technology by experiencing it firsthand through demonstrations, games, and simple experiments. In keeping with that theme, almost everything we cover in this book will be hands-on, putting you right in the middle of the action. So just hang on and have a blast!

INSTALLATION

Let's get down to business and start installing the accompanying software and sound files. Before you begin, read the following hardware and software requirements. A number of the programs will work on systems with only minimal configurations, but some have more stringent requirements.

HARDWARE REQUIREMENTS

Here is the minimum hardware required to run all of the included programs:

- 386 processor or faster; math coprocessor helpful
- Hard disk with 6 megabytes free
- VGA color display
- Microsoft-compatible mouse
- Sound Blaster Pro or true compatible sound card with stereo

In particular, QSound 3-D demos need a stereo sound card, Windows applications need a 386 processor, the PMP mod player needs a VGA display, and the MicFFT program will run faster with a math coprocessor. You can get away with a slightly reduced configuration and still get a lot out of this book. Some of the more important demonstration software (Blaster Master, MicFFT, ASCOPE, WSCOPE) require the following hardware:

- 286 processor

- Hard disk with 1 to 2 megabytes free (assuming only the necessary files for a particular section are on disk)
- EGA display
- Microsoft-compatible mouse (required for Blaster Master)
- Sound Blaster or compatible monophonic sound card

Several of the programs will operate with character mode displays on 8088/8086 processors, but you will not be able to follow along with the majority of material in this book using such a system. Each chapter tells about any special hardware requirements when the programs are introduced.

Although it is possible to use some of this material on a floppy-based system, it's not very practical, so we assume that you have a hard disk system. The two accompanying disks are both high-density, 1.4 megabyte media. All the material is stored in compressed form. To do a full installation from them, you will need approximately 6 megabytes of storage during installation, and a little over 5 megabytes to hold the final set of files. If you do not have that much space available, you can install individual subdirectories from the disks as needed. If you are a Windows user, remember to keep several megabytes in reserve for Windows' temporary space.

SOFTWARE REQUIREMENTS

All of the included programs have been tested under MS-DOS versions 4, 5, and 6. Although most are likely to operate under MS-DOS 3, PC-DOS, and DR DOS, they have not been verified. The Windows applications in Chapter 10 require Microsoft Windows version 3.1 or higher, with all necessary sound drivers installed (see your sound card manual).

INSTALLATION

The Sound Effects Playhouse programs and data files are stored on two floppy disks. To install them on your hard drive, insert Disk 1 in drive A and type:

```
A:INSTALL <ENTER>
```

If you are installing from drive B, type B:INSTALL instead. The INSTALL program performs the steps necessary to copy and expand the distribution files. You should not try to copy them manually.

Before starting the actual installation process, the INSTALL program gives you the opportunity to change certain options. At the top of the screen, you can select the source drive letter (the floppy disk you are installing from), the destination drive letter (the hard drive you are installing to), and the destination directory name (the directory in which you would like the programs and data to be installed). The examples in the book assume that you installed everything in a directory called \SEP, but you are free to choose another name. Use the up and down arrow keys to select these options, and type over the existing options to specify new ones.

The rest of the display contains a list of subdirectories to install. The programs and data for Sound Effects Playhouse are grouped by topic area and are kept in individual subdirectories under the main directory (usually \SEP). Each chapter in the book instructs you to use material from one or more subdirectories. If you are only interested in certain ones (or do not have space to install everything), you can indicate the subdirectories that should not be installed by changing Ⓨ to Ⓝ for those you do not want. Use the up and down arrow keys to select a subdirectory line and type Ⓨ or Ⓝ to change the selection. If you do not select all of the subdirectories to be installed, you may run INSTALL from Disk 1 again at a later time to install additional subdirectories.

After you are done making any changes, press F2 to begin the installation process. When the first disk has been copied, you will be instructed to insert Disk 2 and press ENTER. When both disks have been copied, the program will begin expanding the files in each subdirectory. This process may take some time, so you may want to get a cup of coffee while you're waiting.

SETUP

Several of the directories contain setup programs that make sure the other programs in those directories are properly configured for your hardware. Each section that discusses these programs will direct you to use the appropriate setup program. If, however, you jump right in and try to run the programs, look for a program of the form xxxSETUP.EXE, and if one exists, run it before any of the other programs. For example, the \SEP\SOUND directory contains a setup program called SNDSETUP.EXE. In some cases, you should not run the actual applications directly, but instead, a batch file that has been provided. This is why it is a good idea to read the corresponding sections of the book before running anything.

For most users, the default sound card settings will work without any special setup. The most important settings are port address and IRQ number. If you changed these on your card, be sure you know what they are before running the setup programs. For audio recording and playback, the standard port address is 220. For FM sound, the standard port address is 388. On most Sound Blaster and compatible cards, the IRQ number is 7. On Pro Audio Spectrum cards, the Sound Blaster compatibility option uses IRQ 5 instead, so you may need to identify this change for some of the programs that are expecting a Sound Blaster on IRQ 7.

SOUND CARD COMPATIBILITY

With the exception of a few of the included programs (which specifically support other brands), most assume Sound Blaster or Sound Blaster Pro compatibility. There are many clones on the market—some more compatible than others. Please be sure you are using a 100 percent compatible sound device. In general, the Pro Audio Spectrum line of cards is closely compatible, but you may need to pay special attention to your documentation to assure proper operation. Most of the programs use just the basic capabilities of the sound card, so compatibility is usually not an issue. There are many new cards, however, that try to simulate features of the original cards. These features cannot always be correctly located, or can produce strange results. If you are having difficulty with a particular card, check with your retailer or the company about known compatibility problems.

SHAREWARE

Several of the included demo programs are being distributed as shareware. This means that they are copyrighted, commercial programs, just like those you would buy in any store. The authors have agreed to let us use these programs for demonstration purposes only. If you like any of these programs and continue to use them, you must buy licensed copies to legally keep running them beyond a reasonable evaluation period. Please pay particular attention to those programs noted as shareware, and see the authors' documentation on disk for license terms. In all cases, registering these shareware programs will entitle you to the most recent versions, technical support, and perhaps other bonuses and special offers.

INTRODUCTION

If you're someone who really enjoys sound and music, and you've been using personal computers for a while, you've probably been disappointed by the inability of DOS-based machines to come up with anything but the occasional, annoying beep. You are probably envious of your friends or coworkers with Macs and Amigas because they have sound and you don't. Well that's all changed. It took years, but now there are more options for DOS than anyone can hope to keep straight. For better or worse, the open architecture of the IBM PC and its clones has promoted staggering growth in the computer sound industry. And the latest buzz word, "multimedia," has whipped it all up to a fever pitch. There's no more Mac-envy because of sound, that's for sure!

Although other products preceded it, Creative Lab's Sound Blaster was the sound card that started the revolution. It wasn't necessarily the best—just the first card priced within the reach of most consumers to combine music with audio recording and playback. It took off with a vengeance! As you might suspect, its biggest market was for game applications; finally, the beeps were dead, replaced by realistic voices, sound effects, and full musical scores.

So what else besides games are sound cards good for? Good question. Frankly, a lot of people are still wondering if they really serve any useful purpose. (But not to worry, a lot of those people are still trying to figure out why we need color TVs and stereo recordings.) The answer is that they're not an end unto themselves, they just make the ways in which we interact with our technology more natural. Sound is the first and most natural method of human communication. If music coming from a computer helps us enjoy life,

SOUND EFFECTS PLAYHOUSE

it's good. If gentle audible warnings help us use a program more productively, that's good. If sounds help sell a demonstration program, what's wrong with that? And if we can start talking to our computers like any other assistant—and they talk back—now we're really cooking!

Sound is a natural medium, so the more we use it in computing, the more natural that environment can become. As sound becomes a more popular medium, we get the unavoidable market frenzy that accompanies any popular product. If you look at the sound card market today, it's becoming a lot like the stereo component market. The capability of some sound cards has gone beyond what most people need or want, with exotic features galore. Another of our goals in this book is to give you enough information to evaluate product features and cut through all the hype and glitz. That way you'll be able to make well-informed decisions when buying sound hardware and software.

The market is evolving rapidly. There are sound cards available now that can pretty convincingly stand in for a small orchestra, or be used to record cuts for a commercial-quality CD. We're not going to try to grab that tiger by the tail. We'll be content to explore just the most common denominators among sound cards. After all, most people seldom use all the new features of any high-tech product. And they often ignore even the simplest capabilities because they've been overwhelmed by features. For example, how many times have you seen a VCR with a clock that hasn't been set?

We want you to be able to make the most of your sound card, and to do that, we'll stick with the basics. You'll see how to take control of the different kinds of sound your card can produce, the software tools that make this possible, and hot new products that will have your computer doing the equivalent of back flips. Forget the pathetic beeps and groans you've grown accustomed to and crank up those speakers. You won't want to miss any of it!

OVERVIEW

Starting off with basic audio technology, we'll explore tools to help understand and work with recorded sound. Then we'll move on to some interesting new application areas, including speech and 3-D sounds. Looking at alternate sound creation methods, we'll delve into FM synthesis and see how this old, but still powerful, technique can produce an incredible range of useful sounds. Then we'll take an excursion into some music applications, seeing a few interesting opportunities for using music, and finding ways of stretching your

investment to get sound quality you never expected. Next on the list is getting DOS to speak up and not be so quiet. We'll investigate various methods for attaching sounds to programs and events in DOS to liven it up. Finally, we'll explore the next frontier, Windows, and see a potpourri of hot applications that are making Windows the new environment of choice for multimedia.

The disks included with this book are packed with 2.5 megabytes of great public domain, shareware, and demo programs. Along with the programs, we have included another 2.5 megabytes of music and sound files. There are dozens of songs for your listening pleasure, including traditional, classical, and original pieces. There are also hundreds of ready-made sounds that you can use right away. If you get tired of our sounds, don't worry; we provide all the tools you need to create your own endless supply.

The chapters in the book are summarized here. They are almost all fully hands-on, so you'll probably want to be at your computer while you're reading the book. Each chapter uses one or more programs to demonstrate the topics it covers. For example, Chapter 7 introduces the FM sound process using the SBTimbre program to show you exactly how you can use FM to create exciting new sounds. Some chapters take you through simple tutorials, while others leave you on your own to explore and enjoy the included programs and sound files.

Chapter 1 Digital Audio Basics

- Understand sound by looking as well as listening.

- Use the Audio Scope and MicFFT programs to view sounds and their components.

- See how digital audio is captured and the effects of the process on sound quality.

Chapter 2 Editing And Effects

- Digitally edit sounds to alter reality.

- Learn the basics of the Blaster Master program.

- Cut and paste sounds.

〰 Mix sounds, add "echo," and produce other special effects.

〰 Play and edit over half a megabyte of included sounds.

Chapter 3 Audio Recording

〰 Learn how to set up the recording environment for best results.

〰 Deal with nasty problems such as noise and distortion.

〰 Create your own recordings with Blaster Master.

〰 Control the size of digital recordings.

Chapter 4 Speech

〰 Explore the challenges of getting computers to talk and listen.

〰 Look at real speech using the Word Scope program.

〰 Experiment with voice recognition using the VDEMO voice command game.

Chapter 5 Three-Dimensional Sound

〰 See how we are able to perceive the location of sounds, and how studying this process lets us restore sound direction information in recordings.

〰 Listen to a megabyte of sound clips processed using QSound.

Chapter 6 Sound Synthesis

〰 Solve problems of digitized sound by using your sound card to create new sounds on the fly.

- Explore the process of FM synthesis.

- Listen to sound synthesis in action.

- Use the SBTimbre program to create and edit FM sounds.

- Create new families of sounds through randomizing.

- Learn how to make new sounds and create sound effects.

- Pick and choose from the included library of over 250 FM sounds.

Chapter 7 Music

- Learn about computer-controlled music and MIDI.

- See how to improve the sound quality when listening to song files.

- Play music on your computer while you're running other programs.

- Listen to a half a megabyte of included MIDI song files and music clips.

Chapter 8 Mod Players

- See how sampling technology creates new realism in PC music.

- Use the DMP and PMP programs to play mod files. Included is half a megabyte of original mod format song files.

Chapter 9 Adding Sound to DOS

- Use batch files to add sound effects and music to DOS.

- Look at three kinds of sound and music players.

- Hook into the system and attach FM sound effects to common DOS events.

Chapter 10 Windows Medley

ᴧᴧ　See how Windows multimedia devices operate.

ᴧᴧ　Use the Windows Media Player program to play all kinds of files.

ᴧᴧ　Attach sounds to Windows events using Whoop It Up!

ᴧᴧ　Explore the Windows Sound Recorder.

ᴧᴧ　Edit sounds digitally using Wave Editor.

ᴧᴧ　See Windows command recognition in action with the IN3 demo.

Chapter 11 Taking Inventory

ᴧᴧ　Find tips on locating material in this book.

ᴧᴧ　Sort out the included programs, sound files, and music.

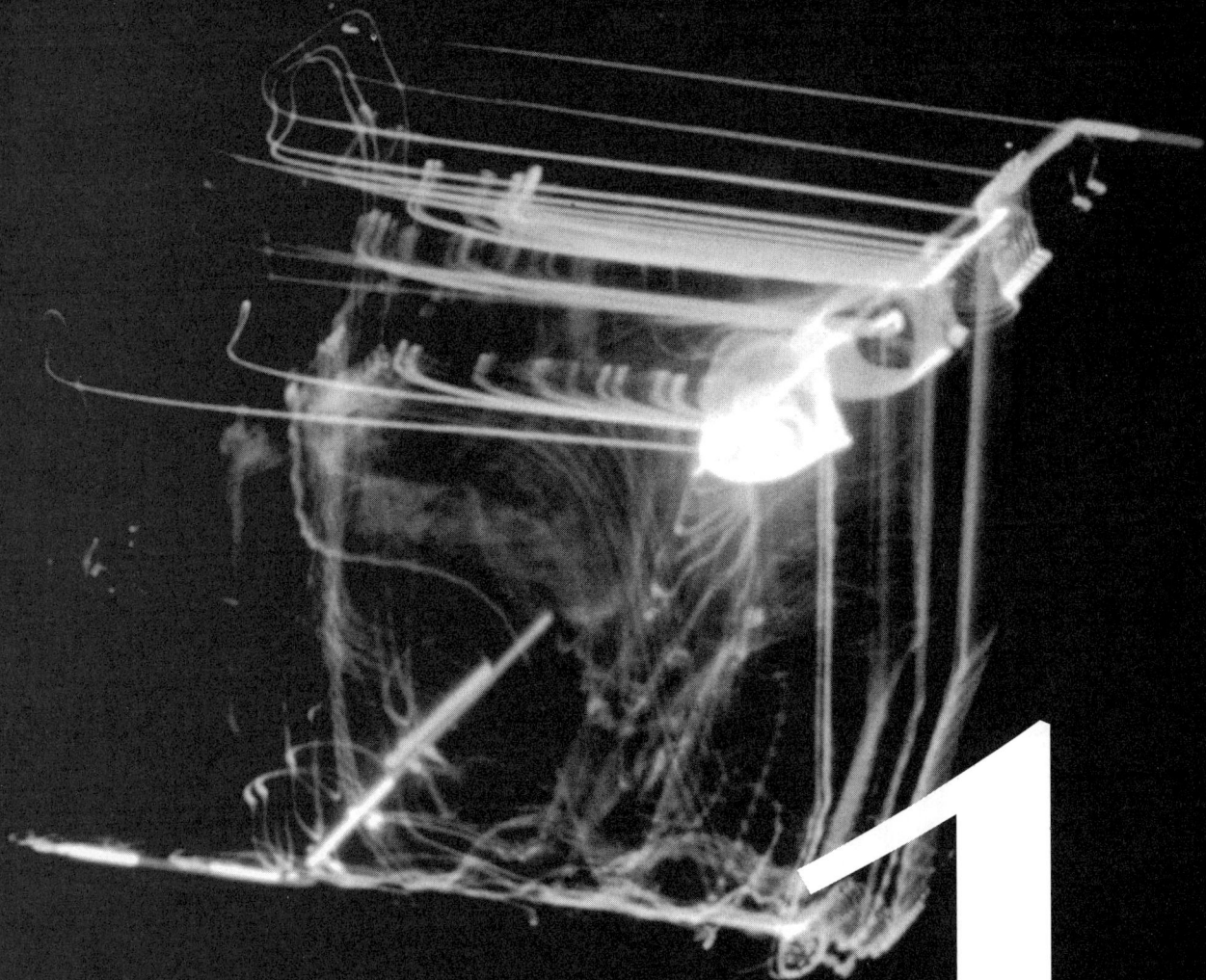

1

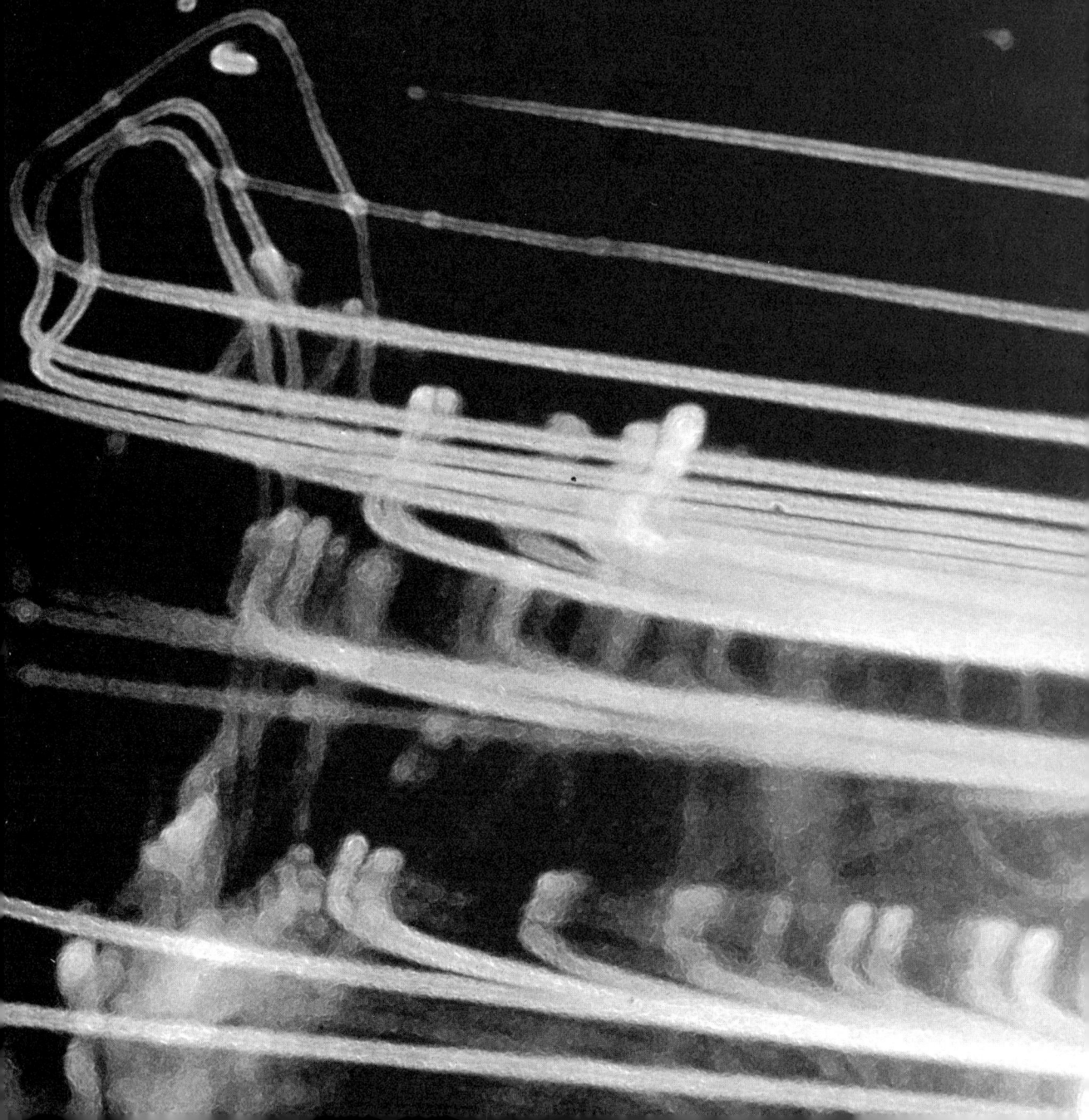

1

Digital Audio Basics

Audio can be a very complex subject, but with a little background, plus the proper tools, you'll soon have your sound card doing some pretty amazing things. Through a series of simple experiments and demonstrations, we'll cover a few key topics in this chapter that you should be familiar with before diving into the rest of the book. You'll find that hearing isn't the only sense you can rely upon when working with sound—computers provide the tools to examine and manipulate it visually as well. We'll look at the process of getting computers to store sound, and why it's perhaps not a very natural thing to try in the first place. But rest assured, we'll do it anyway!

SOUND PROPERTIES

Sound plays a vital role in our lives, but how much do we really know about it? Okay, we know that sound can be loud or soft, low and boomy or high and shrill, smooth or raspy, soothing or gut-wrenching, or noisy and hard to hear. But these are subjective terms. In order to discuss sound more

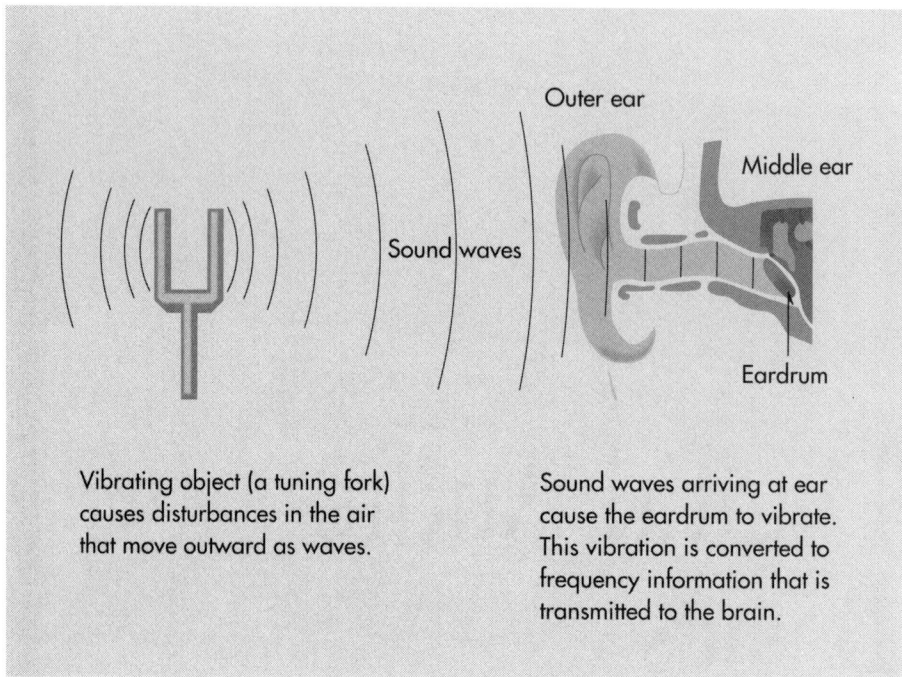

Figure 1-1 A vibrating object causes air movement, which we perceive as sound

objectively, here are a few sound properties to keep in mind as we work through the examples.

Frequency

Frequency refers to the speed of a physical oscillation that causes a sound. If we hear a sound, there's bound to be something vibrating, crashing, or swooshing by. That something is moving the air, sending out waves of sound to our ears. Hearing is the effect of those waves reaching us. More specifically, it's the individual waves causing the air to compress and expand around our ears that causes our eardrums to vibrate, triggering the sensation of sound (see Figure 1-1). How fast the vibration occurs is the sound's frequency, which is measured in cycles per second. We'll be using more modern terminology and referring to cycles per second as hertz (abbreviated Hz), and thousands of

cycles per second as kilohertz (kHz). The term pitch is often used interchange-ably with frequency, though it is not as precise because it describes what we think we hear, which isn't always the same as the sound that was made.

Volume

Volume describes the intensity of a sound. The term loudness is often used instead, but like pitch, it is not as precise. Our ears are less sensitive to volume at certain frequencies. A less scientific argument can also be made that we're more sensitive to volume at different times of the day (see Figure 1-2)! Sound intensity is important in connection with the recording process, where careful attention to volume levels while recording is essential to good sound quality.

Tone

Think about the bass and treble tone controls on a stereo and how they affect the sound. Saying that a sound is dull or bright is one way of describing a sound's tone. Musicians often use the word timbre (pronounced "tamber") instead, to describe the overall feel of a sound. Tone and timbre are frequency properties, true, but they're much more than simply how high or low a sound

Figure 1-2 We can measure volume very precisely, but loudness is more subjective

might be. Sounds change dramatically in a short time, and it's the timbre that ultimately distinguishes a concert piano from crashing glass.

Noise and Distortion

If it weren't for Murphy's Law, the properties just mentioned would be enough to describe most sounds. But, since it's not a perfect world, we tend to get all sorts of nasty additives in the form of noise and distortion. Tune a radio slightly off a particular station and you'll hear examples of both; you'll also have to deal with them as you start doing your own recordings. Noise and distortion can be controlled, however, and it's not always a matter of paying more for better equipment; sometimes just a little care will do the trick.

LISTEN AND LOOK

In this book, we'll be recording sounds and editing them to get the effects we want. In order to manipulate these sounds, you need to get used to the idea that listening isn't always the best way to examine sounds. It's true that you'll probably know the final sound when you hear it, but getting there can be an exercise in frustration. You need to give your poor ears a little help. Fortunately, plenty of tools are available that we can use to "look" at sounds.

Catching a Wave: The Audio Scope Program

SEP\SOUND\
ASCOPE

First, let's look close up at a sound. You'll need a microphone plugged into your sound card for the following examples. Any sound source will actually work, but your voice will produce the most useful results. You'll also need an EGA or VGA display. Be sure to follow the instructions on installing the programs in this book if you haven't already done so. Change to the \SEP\SOUND directory and run the SNDSETUP program before proceeding. Now type ASCOPE and you'll see the Audio Scope screen pictured in Figure 1-3. Audio Scope lets us see a continuous visual representation of the sounds the microphone is picking up.

Pro Audio Spectrum users: If your microphone input is not set to a reasonably high level, follow the instructions in your manual for changing it.

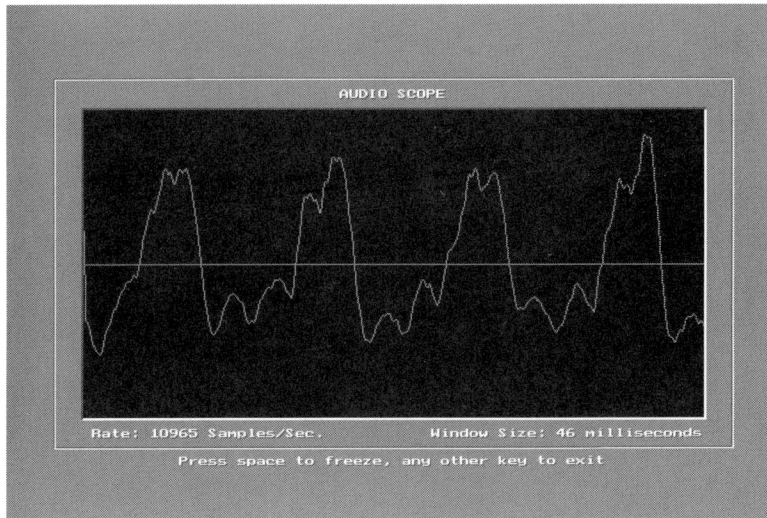

Figure 1-3 Audio Scope's display showing how a computer can help visualize sounds

Okay, now make some noise—yell, whistle, drop the microphone—whatever. Did you notice the jagged line dancing around the horizontal center line? What you're seeing is a series of very small snapshots of the sound being displayed in rapid succession. Depending on the speed of your machine, that may be a few times a second; up to dozens of times on faster machines. The effect is an animated view of the sound.

We referred to sound as an oscillation—waves in the air caused by rapid compression and expansion around a vibrating sound source. Our ears respond to those waves and we hear sound. The microphone responds similarly by converting the air pressure into an electrical current flowing in one direction and then another, corresponding to the pushing and pulling of the waves in the air. What the Audio Scope program presents is a graphical view of that pushing and pulling during a short period of time (the actual length of time is shown beneath the display in milliseconds, or thousandths of a second). As you view the image from left to right, compression of the air makes the line swing above the center line, and expansion of the air makes it swing below the center line. You see this happening repeatedly across the display. You can also see that louder sounds cause a wider swing from top to bottom.

To get a better feel for how this works, start whistling in as low a pitch as you can. Try to keep the pitch uniform, and don't get too close to the microphone. Hold the tone as long as you can (without losing consciousness, of

7

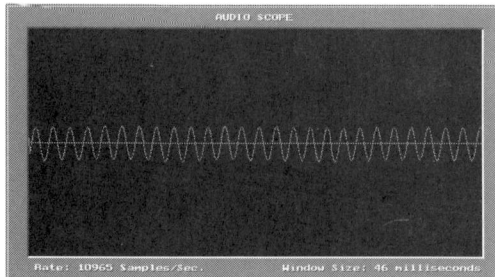

(a) whistle

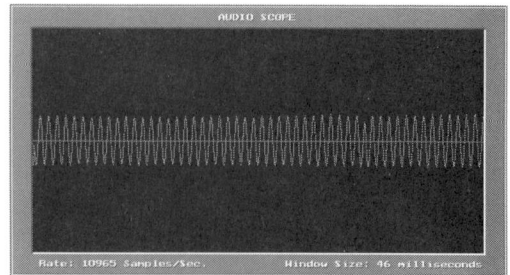

(b) whistle one octave higher

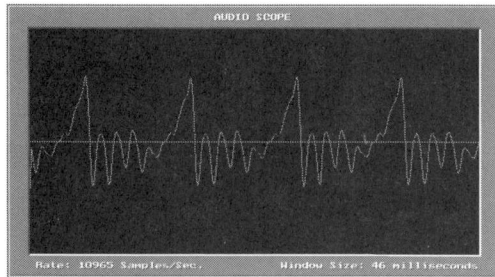

(c) "ahhhhh"

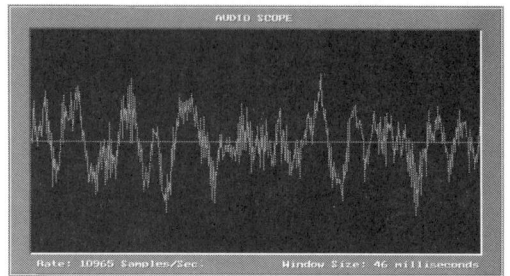

(d) hiss

Figure 1-4 Sample waveforms showing different types of vocal sounds

course). What you'll see is very close to a pure sound wave (see Figure 1-4a). We'll refer to graphical views such as this as waveforms. This particular waveform is approximately what is called in mathematics a sine (or cosine) wave. The sine wave is very important in the study of sound, and we'll be talking more about it later.

Now let's look at the effect of pitch. Keep whistling (okay, you can take a breath first), and gradually raise the pitch. You'll see the peaks of the waves move closer together as the frequency of the sound increases and more oscillations can take place in the same amount of time. If you're musically inclined, increase the pitch in steps as you move through the scale (do, re, mi, fa, sol, la, ti, do). If you do this carefully, you'll notice twice as many peaks by the time you get to the top of the scale (see Figure 1-4b). The octave in music is simply a doubling of the frequency of a note, and you've just proven that graphically.

Let's try a more complex sound. Pretend you're at the doctor's and say "ahhhhh." Not quite as smooth as the whistle, is it? The whistle was very close to a perfect sine wave, or pure tone. When you say "ah," your vocal

tract is actually producing a series of pure tones at different frequencies all at once; they are added together and result in the more irregular waveform you see in Figure 1-4c. There are still peaks, and as you change the pitch of your voice higher or lower, the number of peaks changes.

Finally, try hissing loudly into the microphone (taking care not to pick a fight with any cats). When you do this, there is almost no detectable regularity in the waveform, as you can see in Figure 1-4d. Hissing is mostly noise, and noise is made up of hundreds of pure tones (sine waves) at different frequencies, all adding together randomly.

Go ahead and experiment, making different sounds to see what they look like. Notice in particular how they change over time. A good example is the word "so." Stretch it out and say it very slowly over two or three seconds. You'll see how the "s" part is mostly noise, settling into a more regular waveform as you get to the "o." How sounds change over time will play an important part in our discussions as we progress through the book.

SEP\SOUND\MF

Breaking it Down: The MicFFT Program

Looking at waveforms gives us a lot of information about sounds, but it's not always enough. We talked about sounds often being composed of many simpler, pure tones. Finding out the frequency and intensity of those individual tones can be very helpful in understanding sounds. In this section, we'll be using a great little program by Craig Walsh called MicFFT to do spectrum analysis. Just as the light spectrum can be broken down into individual colors of the rainbow using a prism, so can sounds be broken down into simpler tones. A mathematical procedure called the Fourier Transform can extract this information from a waveform. A programmed method of doing this quickly on computers is known as the Fast Fourier Transform, or FFT. The MicFFT program continuously processes sound input using the FFT, and displays the frequency breakdown of sounds in real time. To run the program, type MF. After the program starts up, press the (SPACEBAR) to begin the analysis.

Just as the Audio Scope program in the last section showed an animated view of a waveform, MicFFT shows an animated view of the sound's spectrum, or frequency makeup (see Figure 1-5). If you go back and do the same sound experiments from the last section you'll see how it works.

First, try whistling. Notice the large peak showing the primary frequency component of the tone. Changing the pitch, you can see the peak move to the

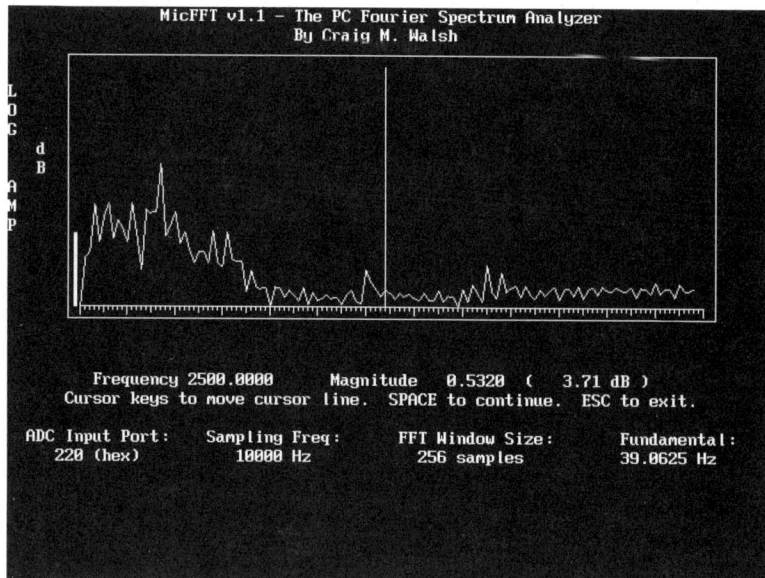

Figure 1-5 MicFFT's display showing sounds
broken down into component frequencies

right as it rises, or to the left as it drops. The cleaner you can make the tone, the sharper and more distinct the peak will be.

Try "ahhhhh" again. As you recall, that gave us a slightly more irregular waveform. Now you can see the reason: There are several peaks corresponding to the multiple tones making up the sound. Next, try hissing again. Notice the wider spread of many small peaks? This kind of spread across the spectrum is characteristic of noise. If you go back to whistling, and gradually move closer to the microphone, the hissing of the air around the mouthpiece will add noise to the otherwise fairly clean tone.

As before, pay particular attention to the way the spectrum changes over time. Try out various words, speaking them slowly and seeing how they change. If you play a musical instrument, try playing it into the microphone to see what it looks like.

If you have a sound source connected, such as a stereo, look at some music. Try changing its tone controls. Notice what happens when you add bass: The left side of the display gets higher and thicker as the lower bass frequencies come in, as shown in Figure 1-6a. Then try the treble control and watch the way the higher frequencies on the right are emphasized, as in Figure 1-6b.

10

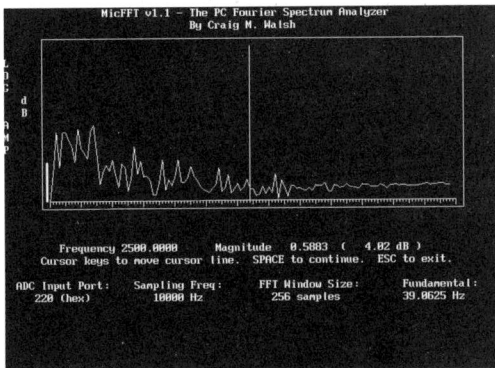

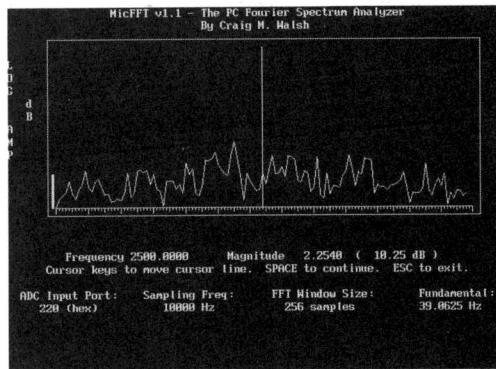

(a) bass emphasized
(b) treble emphasized

Figure 1-6 Watching the effects of a stereo's bass and treble controls

Zooming Back Out

In the last two sections, we looked at sounds during short instants of time. We saw that there were many rapid changes—too rapid to really get a good handle on the sounds. Let's pull back a little and look at some sounds over longer periods of time. The next few images were prepared using a professional sound tool from Turtle Beach Systems called Wave for Windows (not included with this book). First we'll examine a note being played on a cello. The cello (pronounced "chello") is a large, deep sounding member of the violin family

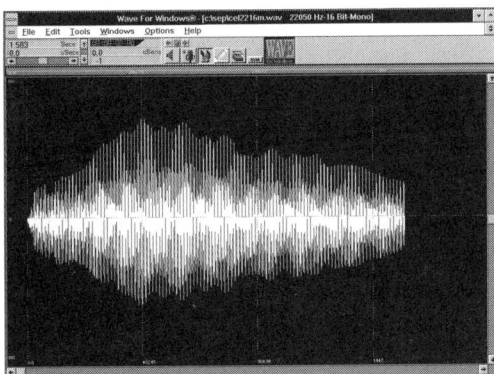

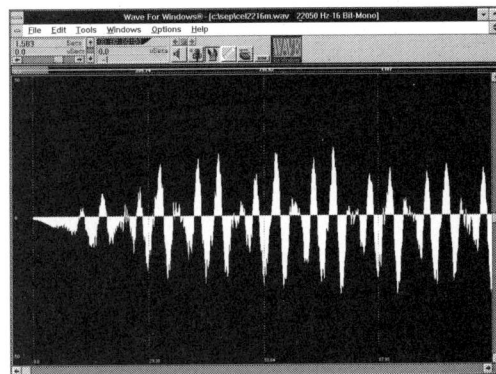

(a) 1.6 seconds
(b) 0.1 second

Figure 1-7 Viewing a cello's waveform to get clues about the sound

11

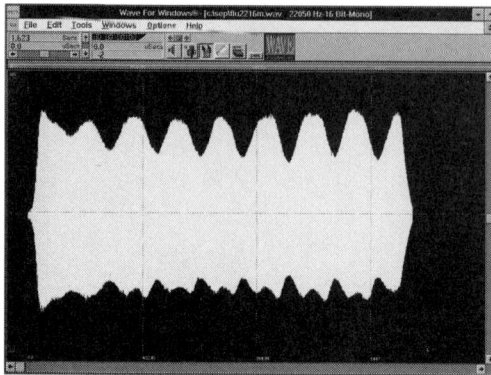
(a) 1.6 seconds

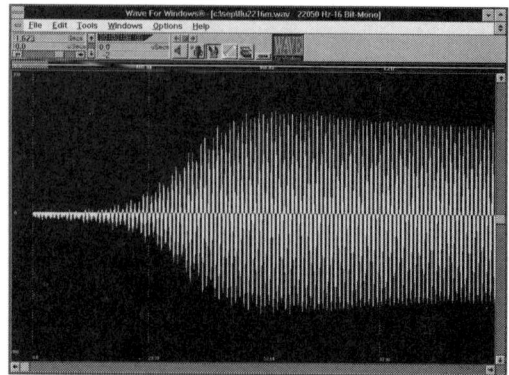
(b) 0.1 second

Figure 1-8 Looking at a flute's waveform to see how it differs from the cello

that stands upright and is played with a bow. Run CELLO to listen to its sound (type CELLO and press (ENTER)).

Figure 1-7a shows 1.6 seconds of the cello's waveform. Because of the fairly low frequency, we can still see some detail in the oscillations. We can also see some larger dips along the top and bottom edges of the waveform; this is showing tremolo, or a slow variation in the loudness. Where the waveform thickens and spreads out, we see the effects of vibrato, or a slow change in the sound's pitch. Looking at just the first tenth of a second in Figure 1-7b, we can see how the sound rises. This is the sound's attack, and for the cello, it's relatively slow. The vertical scale on this plot was also increased for easier viewing—you're actually just seeing the tiny nub on the left of the first plot, so it's pretty obvious that it takes a long time for the sound to build. We'll be talking more about attack and similar sound attributes in later chapters.

For a slightly different sound, run FLUTE to hear 1.6 seconds of a flute being played. Now look at its waveform in Figure 1-8a. Notice that it has completely blurred together because of its higher frequency components. Figure 1-8b shows the first tenth of a second. Here, the attack is much shorter, so the tone begins almost immediately at full volume.

We'll be seeing more of this kind of waveform in the next two chapters as we start recording and modifying sounds. But we also need to think about how the frequency makeup of these sounds changes over time. Let's see how the sample tones appear if we take a series of spectrum plots and combine them in a single three-dimensional image. Figure 1-9, also produced using Wave for Windows, shows the cello. This plot shows time (starting at 0 sec-

12

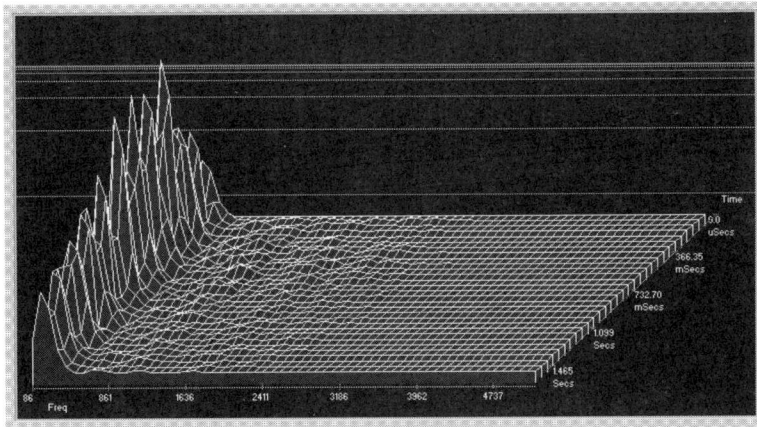

Figure 1-9 A different view of a cello sound—breaking down its frequency components over time

onds) coming out of the page. Frequency is plotted across the page horizontally, and intensity is shown vertically. Each layer moving out of the page is what we saw during a single instant in MicFFT, but now all stacked up. We can see the sound has a strong frequency component that shows up as a big ridge at around 100 Hz. That falls off in intensity as the sound continues. There's not much in the way of high frequencies.

Now look at the flute in Figure 1-10. Notice the parallel ridges at multiples of the base frequency of about 900 Hz. The interesting thing is that they're so

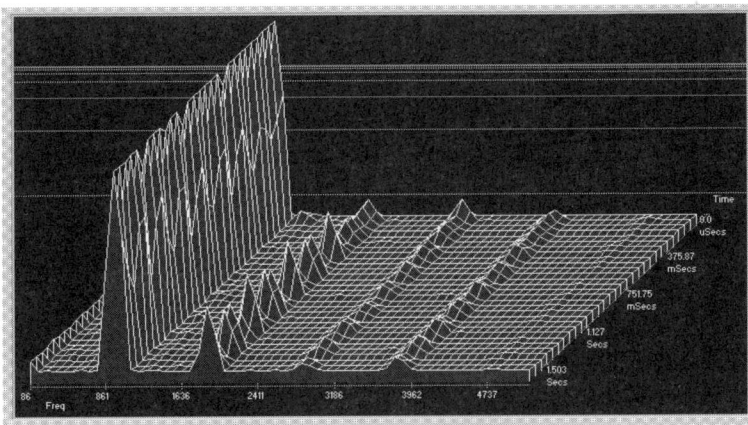

Figure 1-10 The flute's frequency spectrum over time—notice the parallel ridges

pronounced. We talked about timbre early in this chapter. One of the things that gives the flute its timbre, or characteristic sound, is the combination of these relatively strong components at higher frequencies. When recording or processing sound, we need to give some thought to how frequencies are distributed to avoid losing this important information. Chopping off those higher flute frequencies, for example, would destroy the overall quality of the sound, making it much less flutelike.

SAMPLING

We've talked about the basic properties of sound, listened to them, looked at them, and made noises we might not want our friends to know about. Before we go on and do some slicing and dicing of sounds, we have to talk about all the funny business that goes on before a sound ever gets to your computer's memory. Sound in the air is continuously changing, and when it gets convert-

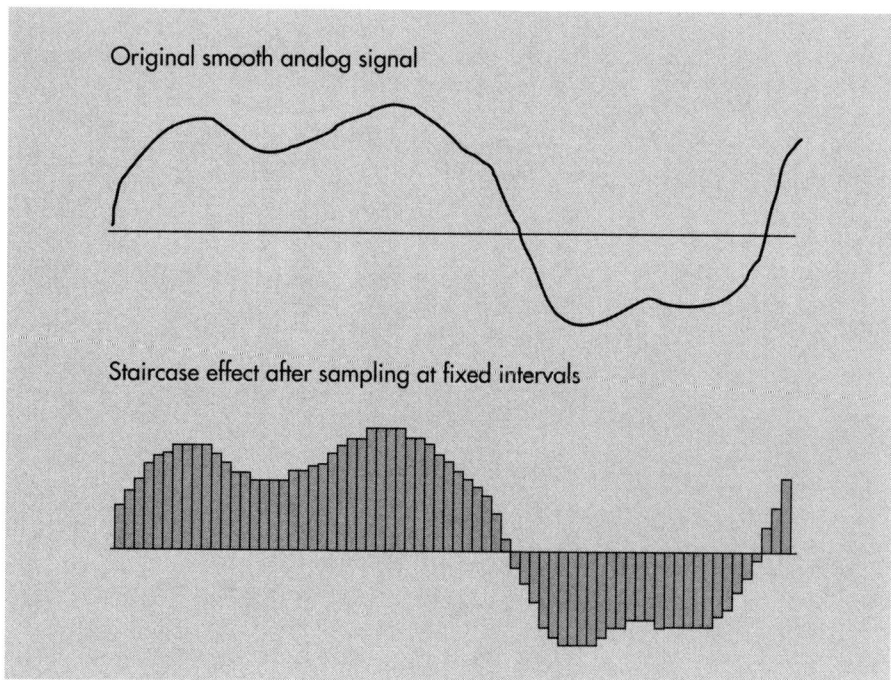

Original smooth analog signal

Staircase effect after sampling at fixed intervals

Figure 1-11 Capturing a sound by taking small, quick snapshots (samples)

14

ed to an electrical signal, the changes are still continuous. Your computer, however, can only store numbers using a limited number of digits of precision. Continuously varying sound is called an analog signal. Once the computer grabs the sound, it doesn't have enough precision to store all the information about the sound in order to perfectly reproduce it. What the computer has stored is called a digital signal representation.

Your sound card captures information about an analog sound signal by measuring its intensity at a given instant. This corresponds to one single point on the waveforms we've been looking at. In order to capture an entire waveform, the measurement process must be repeated at a high rate, usually thousands of times a second. Since the hardware has limited speed and memory capacity, there are only so many points it can capture. Any information between those points is lost forever (but that's not always a problem, as we'll see). Figure 1-11 shows a continuous waveform and how a series of snapshots lets us get an approximation in little chunks that give a kind of staircase effect. This process of capturing the sound in small intervals is called sampling.

To play back a sound, we just reverse the process and convert the digital samples back to an analog signal. Of course, the new signal will probably retain some of the staircase effect, so the reproduction won't be perfect. Figure 1-12 shows the entire process.

Sampling Rate

So just how many points do we need? If you look at audio specs much, you've seen CD sampling rates of 44.1 kHz, or 44,100 samples per second. That's a lot of points! A well-known signal processing theorem (sometimes called the Nyquist Theorem) says that to accurately reproduce a signal, you have to sample at a rate at least twice the highest frequency component in the signal. So the CD sampling rate of 44.1 kHz will capture frequencies up to 22 kHz (a little past the 20 kHz spec that most audio components try to achieve). Of course, most personal computers have trouble doing something a few thousand times a second, let alone tens of thousands, so high-end stereo quality is usually reserved for the fastest machines and most expensive sound cards.

Fortunately, many applications don't require a wide frequency range to get the reproduced sound "good enough." Human speech, for example, contains some frequencies in the 10 kHz range (needing a sampling rate of 20 kHz), but even at 4 kHz (8 kHz sampling), voice is perfectly understandable.

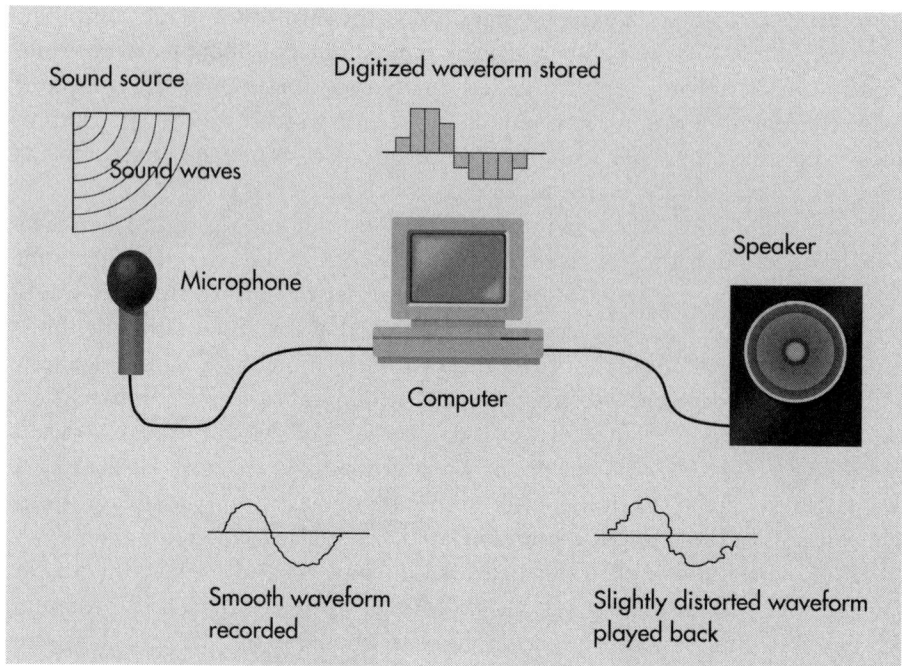

Figure 1-12 Converting a sound to digital form, storing it on a computer, and playing it back

Telephone systems rely on that fact; if they had to handle hi-fi audio, few people could afford the price of phone service.

You might be wondering what happens if you don't sample at a high enough frequency. Well, what you get is something called aliasing. This sinister sounding term just means that since the sample points aren't close enough together, it looks as though you sampled a lower frequency that really wasn't part of the original signal. Alias frequencies are like ghosts—poltergeists really—you can't see them but they make a lot of noise. So by sampling at too low a rate, not only do you miss some of the high frequencies, some of them get thrown back into the mix as unwanted guests at lower frequencies. They are audible as background noise and distortion.

To get a feel for the effect of sampling rate, run RATEDEMO. It plays a sound originally sampled at 11 kHz, showing how it would have sounded if it had been sampled at lower rates. This is an extreme example, but it gets the point across. Notice how the higher frequencies get lost and the voice eventually ends up slurred and distorted.

16

Sampling Resolution

Along with the sampling rate, the other key factor in audio sampling is resolution. Personal computers are designed to work with chunks of data in 8-bit bytes. Because of that, it's convenient for sound cards to use a single byte to represent one sound sample. But because the original sound is a continuous analog signal with an infinite range of loudness levels possible, something's got to give. After all, the 256 possible loudness levels that an 8-bit byte can represent are a lot less than infinite, so you end up with the staircase effect you saw in Figure 1-11. If you looked closely at the screen when you were doing the Audio Scope examples, you may have noticed the squaring off of what should have been smooth waveforms. The visual appearance was partly due to the screen's limited resolution, which is a similar type of problem.

This step effect means that for the time interval of one sample, we're assuming that the waveform was flat, instead of whatever it might have been doing in reality. Squared off waves are legitimate waveforms, but if those sharp edges existed in nature, they would be produced by some pretty nasty high frequencies in the sound. So when we play back the sound, we'll be creating those new frequencies, and they'll sound like background noise.

Noise is the main effect of using a low number of bits to represent sound samples. In audio terminology, we talk about the signal to noise ratio, or SNR of sound equipment. This is a number you get when you divide the maximum sound level by the noise level. You want that number to be as high as possible, indicating that the noise level is very small. The SNR is measured in units of decibels (dB). Decibels are like the Richter scale for measuring earthquake intensity—each step represents a much larger increase than the last. Table 1-1 shows how the number of bits used to store a sample relates to the signal to noise ratio. This table is based on the approximation that each bit is worth 6 dB.

Number of Bits	Signal to Noise Ratio (dB)
4	24
6	36
8	48
10	60
12	72
14	84
16	96

Table 1-1 Bits of resolution versus signal to noise ratio

Don't forget that decibels do not increase at a constant rate. The difference between 8 and 16 bits is not just a simple doubling of the signal to noise ratio. The difference in the noise levels is really a factor of 256!

To listen to the effect of the number of bits on audio quality, run BITDEMO. This plays the same sound clip heard in RATEDEMO, but at different bit resolutions, from 8 bits down to 1. At first, you may not notice much change, except for more background noise at 7 and 6 bits, but by the time you get down to the lowest number of bits, the noise and distortion are extreme. It might be surprising to note, however, that it is still possible to make out the voice using only 1 bit. This might lead you to conclude that the sampling rate is more important than the resolution, and in some cases, that is true. But it's usually best to balance the two, and we'll talk more about that in Chapter 3 when we look at recording in more detail.

CONCLUSION

We've seen how looking at sounds can go a long way in explaining things that might be hard to hear, or at least help us in talking about what we hear. The waveform display is a powerful tool for getting the overall feel of a sound, while spectrum displays go even further by breaking down a sound into its

component frequencies. The more ways we have of looking at something, the better our chances of controlling it.

Moving from real sounds to recorded ones can be a daunting process, with the capabilities of the hardware seriously cramping our style. We saw how the sampling process, in taking away parts of our sound, can actually leave us with more than we started with: uninvited sonic guests. The more we understand sound and the sampling process, the more successful we'll be in keeping those unwanted visitors away.

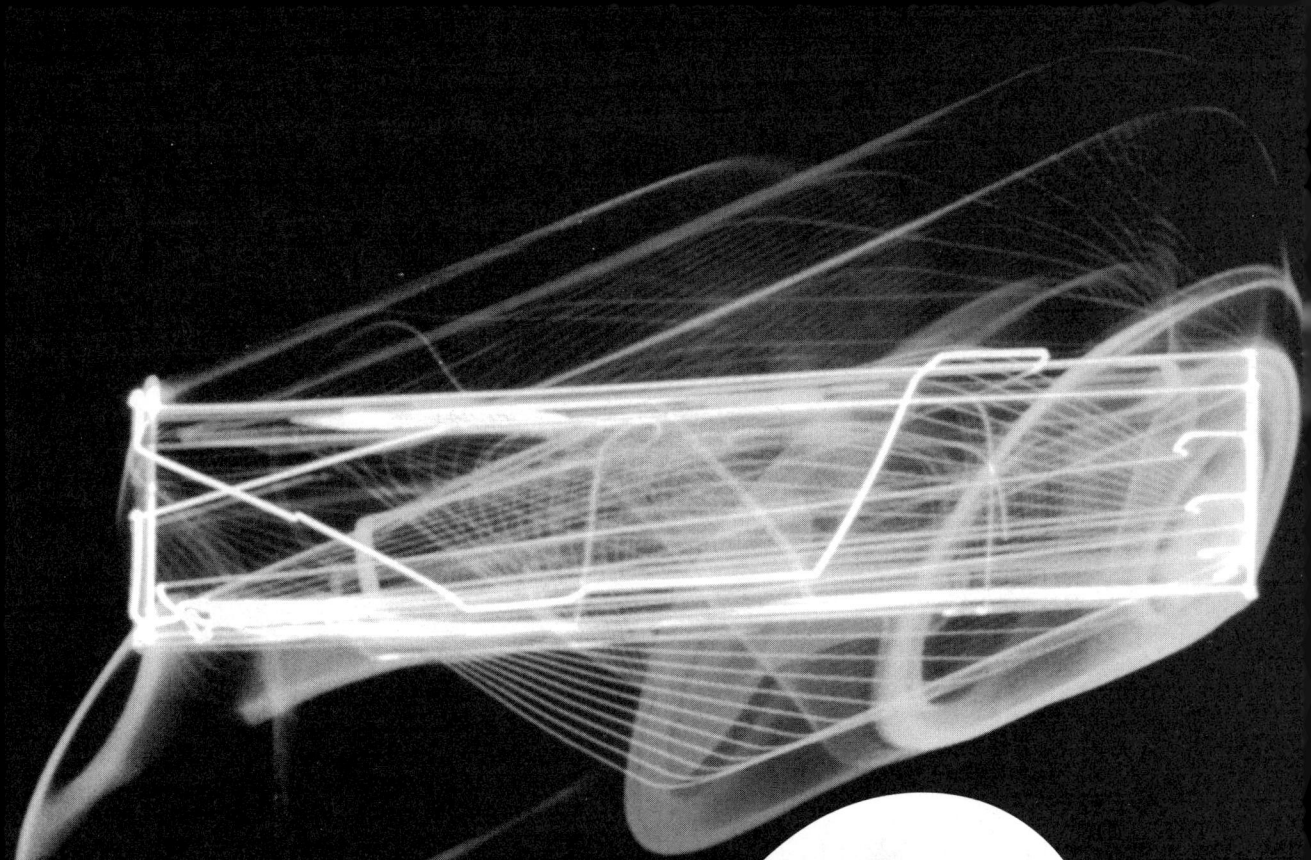

2

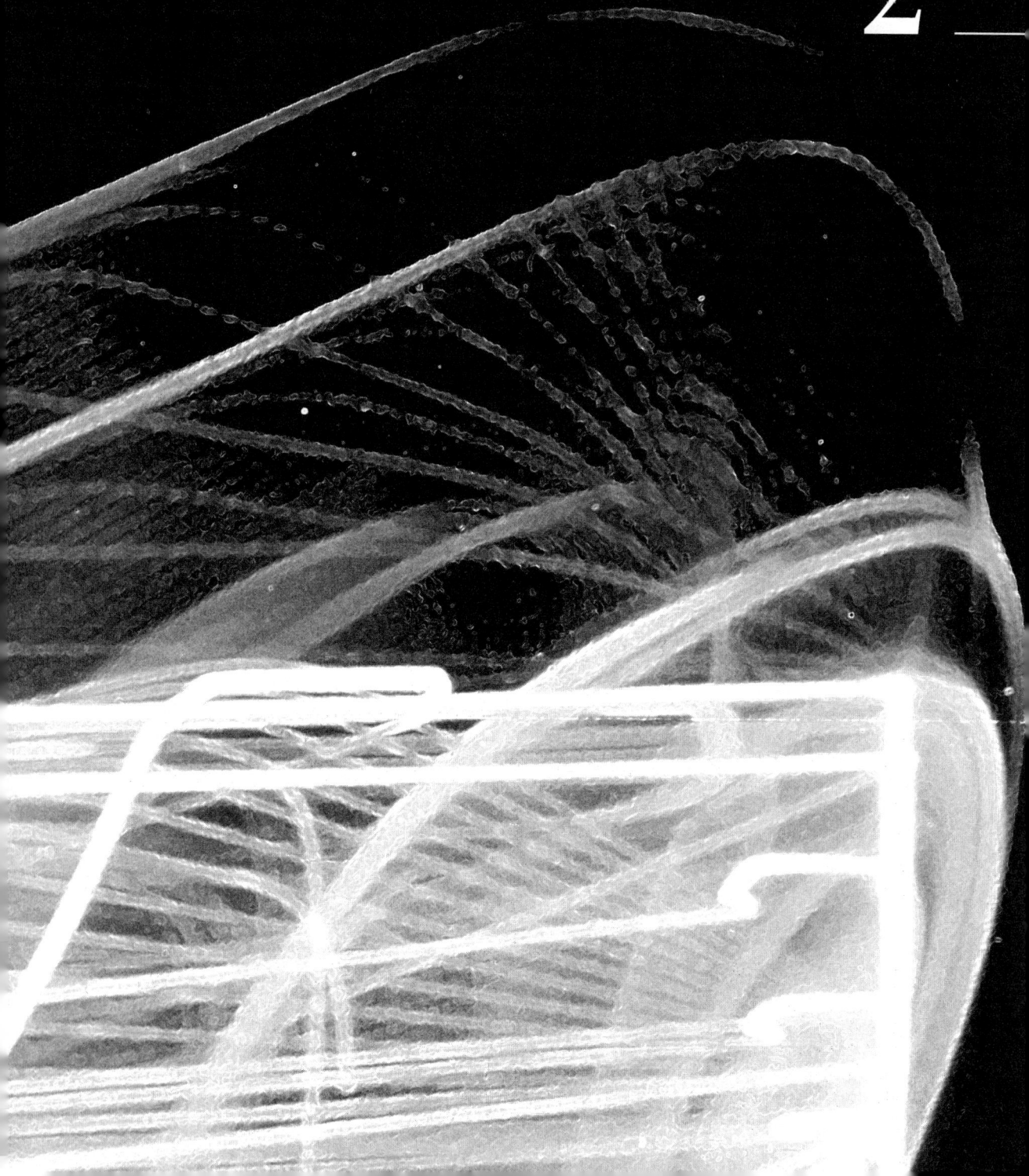

Editing and Effects

You have probably seen at least one movie where the bad guys spliced together a tape from some rather innocent audio clips in order to incriminate one of the stars. These days, it's not necessary to spend hours fussing with tape—the bad guys can do it all on a computer. And the good guys aren't too happy! In this chapter, we'll use digital sound editing to show how this is accomplished and, in the process, rewrite a bit of history. To get the job done, we'll employ the sound editor Blaster Master, a fine shareware program written by Gary Maddox. Not only can it edit sounds, but it can also change their basic texture for some stunning special effects. With tools like this at your disposal, no sound will ever be safe again!

SLICE AND DICE

We'll start off with some basic editing operations, much like those you use in a word processor. Our goal is to take a simple spoken phrase and rearrange it a little. The unfortunate subject of our attack will be the famous utterance by Neil Armstrong as he stepped onto the moon: "That's one small step for man...." To lighten that up a bit, we'll change it to "Man, that's one step!" Then we'll make some other interesting changes—no disrespect meant, of course.

Getting Started with Blaster Master

First to introduce you to Blaster Master, we will cover the program just enough to accomplish what we need to do. Blaster Master is accompanied by full documentation, so you can try out its other features later. To run the program, change to the \SEP\BMSTR directory and type BMASTER. You need to be running on at least a 286 processor and have an EGA or VGA display. Although many operations can be done from the keyboard, a mouse is also required to work through the exercises.

Note: This evaluation copy of Blaster Master will display a registration reminder message at certain points. When it does, press (ENTER) *to proceed.*

Shareware Notice

Blaster Master has been generously provided by Gary Maddox to help in presenting key audio concepts in this book. This is a shareware program, however, so if you like it and continue to use it, you are required to purchase a registered copy. See the files \SEP\BMSTR\BMASTER.DOC and REGISTER.FRM for more information.

On startup, Blaster Master displays a file selection screen. Here you see several files ending with the .VOC extension, as shown in Figure 2-1. VOC (or voice) files are in the native Sound Blaster sound file format. The files shown are located in the current directory. You can choose other drives and directories in the selection box on the right. If you have a mouse, just click directly on items you want to select. Otherwise, you can use the (TAB) and arrow keys to move around the screen. Here, and on other Blaster Master screens, you can "click" a button from the keyboard by pressing (ALT), plus the first letter of the button label (for example, (ALT)-(P) for Play). If the button is highlighted, press (ENTER) to perform the selected function.

The buttons at the bottom of the file window are for common file operations. If you have selected a file, Play will let you audition it without actually loading it in for editing. Record puts Blaster Master in recording mode, which we'll get to in the next chapter. Delete is a utility function to remove sound files. Import is a handy function for loading files that are not in VOC

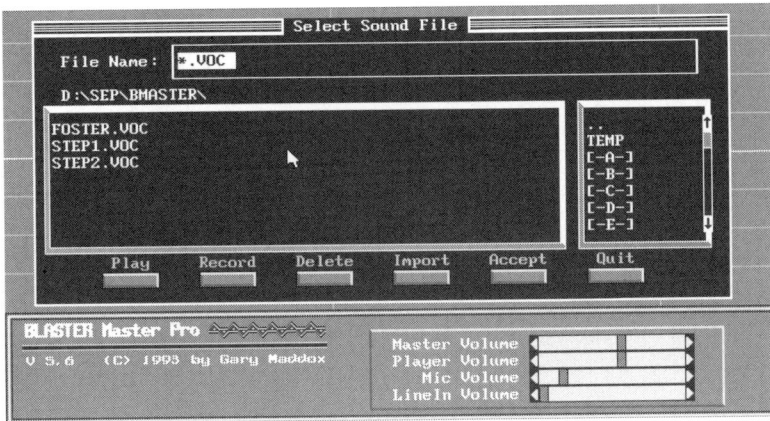

Figure 2-1 Blaster Master's file selection screen

format. Quit exits the program. The Accept button is the one we'll use now to load the selected file for editing. To start, select the file STEP1.VOC and click Accept.

You should now see the main editing screen, as shown in Figure 2-2. In the lower-left corner is information about the file, including its size in bytes, sampling rate in samples per second, total playing length in seconds, and current position. Move the mouse cursor around in the upper wave display section of the screen and notice how the current position (next to Playing Time) changes as you move left and right. We'll be using this indicator to more accurately locate editing points.

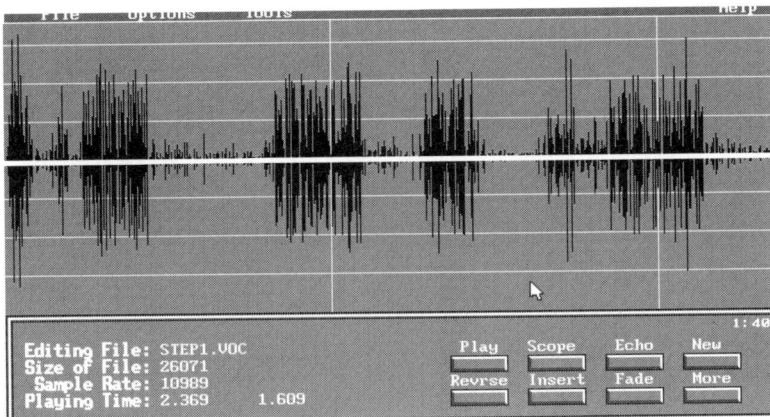

Figure 2-2 Blaster Master's editing screen showing a speech waveform

25

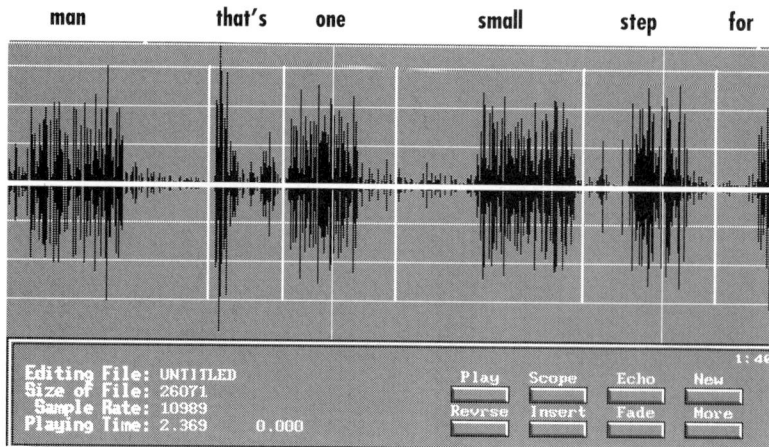

Figure 2-3 Display of sample phrase after moving "man"

The buttons in the lower right perform common editor functions. The More button (when it appears) displays an alternate set of buttons with additional functions. For now, just click on the Play button to listen to the sound clip. As it plays, a vertical line moves across the waveform to show the current play position. Play the file a number of times until you have a good idea of which blips on the screen correspond to the individual words.

Block Editing

Now we're ready to do some rearranging. Recall that what we want to do is change the phrase from "That's one small step for man" to "Man, that's one step." First, we'll move "man" from the end to the beginning. Move your cursor along the waveform until the position indicator reads about 1.794 (seconds). This is approximately where the word "man" starts. Click the left mouse button at that point to select the start of the block. A vertical line appears at that point, and the program asks for a second mark point. Move the cursor all the way to the right edge of the display and click again. You have now blocked "man." Click on Play to listen to it. If you missed, click on New to clear the block and try again until what you have selected sounds right.

To move the block, click on Move, and when asked to select a move point, move the cursor all the way to the left of the waveform and click. Figure 2-3 shows "man" already moved, plus the rest of the words labeled for your reference. Click on Play, and you should hear "Man, that's one small step for."

Now block "for" at the end by selecting a mark point near 2.180, and another all the way at the right edge. Listen to make sure you're not marking too much, and then click on Cut to remove the blocked "for." Finally, cut the word "small." Block the section from about 1.252 to 1.752 and click Cut to remove it. You should now have the complete, modified phrase. If you had any trouble, you can click on New to get to the file selection screen and load in file STEP2.VOC, which contains the complete revision.

Blaster Master also has an alternate pull-down menu for many of its functions. To get to this menu, move the cursor all the way to the top of the screen. This displays a menu bar with File (or Block), Options, Tools, and Help items. Most of these functions are available through the buttons at the bottom, but there are some useful new functions on the pull-down menus. For example, when you have a block marked, there is a Save option on the Block pull-down menu that lets you save just the marked area to a new file. This is especially useful for saving pieces from multiple files and then combining them later using the Insert button to place them at particular points in another sound file.

JUST FOR EFFECT

Next, we'll try out some of Blaster Master's signal processing functions. These go beyond simple cut and paste editing, and actually change the sound for special effects. With these functions, we can mix sounds, produce echoes, fade in and out, speed up or slow down, play sounds backwards (useful for decoding old Beatles albums), and create some other really bizarre effects.

Volume and Mixing

One very common sound file operation is mixing, or overdubbing, one sound file with another. You might want to do this, for example, to add background music to a narration. To try this, let's go back to our original lunar sound clip and see if we can add a bit of the old pioneer spirit with some music. If you're not already in Blaster Master, run it now; otherwise, click on New to get to the file selection screen. Choose the file FOSTER.VOC and load it for editing by clicking Accept. Go ahead and play the sample; you'll probably recognize it as an excerpt from Stephen Foster's "Oh! Susanna."

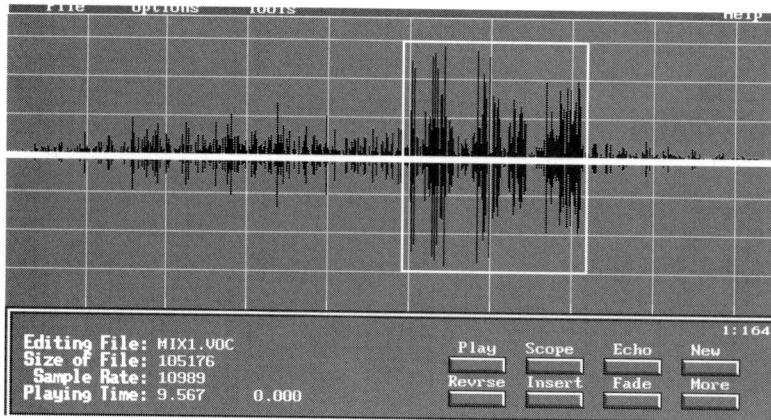

Figure 2-4 Display of background music mixed with voice

The first thing to do is reduce the volume a little, say to 60 percent, so it's not too overpowering. Click the More button to see additional function buttons and then click Volume. When prompted, press (D) and then (ENTER) to decrease the volume, then type 60 and press (ENTER) to select a volume level that is 60 percent of the original.

Next, for a more dramatic effect, we'll fade the music in and out. We have to do this in two steps. Click on the Fade button, and then at the prompt, type 2 for the number of seconds to fade in, and press (ENTER) twice to begin the processing. After the fade-in is complete, click on Fade again. This time press (ENTER) to skip the fade-in, and type 5 and press (ENTER) to fade out the last 5 seconds (4.78 is actually the most the program will use for this file, or one-half its length).

Now that our background music is prepared, it's time to add the voice clip using the mixing function. To identify the location for mixing the clip, move the cursor to about 5 seconds and click the right mouse button. The right button places a triangular reference marker at that point in the wave display. Click the More button and then Mixer; this brings up the file selection screen. Select STEP1.VOC and click Accept. The program will ask for a relative volume to use for the file being mixed in; type 100 (for 100 percent of the original volume) and press (ENTER). You are then asked to select a method for identifying the mix point. We just set a marker for that purpose, so click on By Marker. That should do it; play the file and see how it sounds. Figure 2-4 shows the final waveform. You can see the music fading in and out, plus the point where the speech (shown boxed) comes in. Okay, so maybe there weren't any banjos on the moon, but we can pretend.

Echo

Let's revise history just one more time. Load the sound file STEP2.VOC, our rearranged version of Armstrong's speech. Everyone's always telling you to watch out for that first step, so let's see what would have happened if our moon walker hadn't been so lucky. Click on the waveform at about 1.25 seconds, and again at the right edge to mark a block that includes the word "step." Play it to make sure you got the whole word. Now click on Tools and pick Echo. We're going to reproduce part of the sound and mix it back in a short time later. At the prompt, enter 200 for the delay time (200 milliseconds, or 2/10 of a second) and 70 (percent) for the delay volume. This gives us a delayed, and somewhat softer, copy of the word. Now we'll repeat the process to overlay another echo on top of the first one: mark from 1.25 to the end, choose Tools/Echo; but this time, enter 300 and 50 for the delay time and volume. Just to emphasize the effect, you might want to fade out the last 1 second, as explained earlier. If you haven't listened to the revision yet, try it now and you'll hear our unfortunate astronaut echoing down into the abyss after that first big step!

In most cases, you wouldn't use such extreme delay times and echo volumes. Usually, delays shorter than 200 milliseconds and 10 to 30 percent volumes will give a natural sense of spaciousness. Adding echo and reverberation (multiple echoes), to an otherwise dry sound can give it new life and a more professional feel.

Other Effects

Blaster Master has quite a number of effects, or processing tools, that you can use to enhance or modify your sound files. Most of these are included in the set of function buttons, or you can find them in the pull-down menu under Tools. One effect that can produce strange and unexpected results is the Reverse function. Try that on speech for an amusing diversion, or even on music, and you might discover some interesting new melodies. Most everyday sounds become quite extraordinary when played backwards.

Do you have a clip that's too long but you don't want to cut any of it? Try the Fast function; it speeds up the sound without affecting its pitch. Use the Slow function to do the opposite. Want to change the pitch too? Use the Pitch function and get anything from Darth Vader to Alvin the Chipmunk. There

are even some unique functions that work on stereo sounds to let you remove vocal or rhythm tracks from recorded music.

Raw Material

We've provided a collection of sound files that you can use for experimenting. They are in the \SEP\VOC directory, and they all have an extension of .VOC. You can load any of these files into Blaster Master. Just change the directory on the Blaster Master file selection screen to \SEP\VOC and double-click on any of the .VOC files you see. They are mostly short, special effects clips such as a jet engine, barking dog, whistling bird, and crashing car. Try using some of Blaster Master's special effects and editing functions to change and combine these sounds. For example, you could make multiple copies of a barking dog (BARK.VOC), change the pitch and volume of some of the copies, mix them back together randomly, and end up with a whole kennel full of barking dogs! There are really no limits to what you can create.

CONCLUSION

We've seen how careful digital editing can take reality and completely twist it around. And it's not much more difficult than working with a word processor. Cutting and pasting are simple operations, and creating an echo isn't much harder than selecting a text font. We'll explore more of Blaster Master in the next chapter, but for now, don't be afraid to experiment. The best way to master digital editing is to jump in and let your imagination run wild. You'll soon get a feel for what works well and what to avoid. Digital editing is a powerful tool that gives us a lot of control over sound, but it does take some practice to master.

3

Audio Recording

We spent the last chapter getting comfortable with Blaster Master. It's a lot of fun working on canned sound clips, but sooner or later, you'll get bored with the same old material and want to record your own sounds. Maybe you'd like your computer to start up every day playing some old "I Love Lucy" clips, or if you're a "Star Trek" fan, maybe you'd like a "Beam me up, Scotty" at your fingertips for those times you feel like escaping. The first step is recording real sounds to disk. If you've already tried doing this, you may have been frustrated by poor sound that wasn't nearly the quality you know your sound card is capable of producing. This is a very common experience and often easily remedied with a little care. In this chapter, we'll look at the basic recording process and see how to avoid some of the pitfalls and problems.

RECORDING SETUP

It's easy to get good results when recording audio, but it's even easier to get bad results. Before we start recording, here are a few simple rules to keep in mind:

- Plug into the right jack.
- Watch your volume.

꙳ Avoid using a microphone directly.

꙳ Be patient.

Plug into the right jack

While this may seem obvious, some sound cards have multiple input and output jacks. Now is a good time to review your manual and make sure you know which is which. Plugging a microphone into an output jack is a futile effort, and plugging it into the wrong card is even less productive!

If your sound card has both a microphone and a line input, make sure you know the difference. Typical stereo equipment—tape decks, tuners, CD players—are usually line level devices. Do *not* plug an output marked "speaker" on any of these devices into your sound card; speaker outputs usually operate at high power and may blow out your sound card's circuitry. Only use the jacks marked "line out," "record out," "preamp out," or something similar (check the audio component manual if you have any questions about the particular jacks). These outputs should go to your sound card's *line* input. Plug a microphone only into the *mic* input; it will probably work poorly, or not at all, if plugged into the line input.

What's the difference? It's a matter of voltage. The sound signal is flowing as an electrical current between your sound source and the sound card. The level, or strength, of the signal is measured in volts. Most line level sources are between 0.5 and 2.0 volts. The output level from a microphone is measured in thousandths of a volt, and so requires special circuitry to amplify the signal. If you must plug a line level source into a microphone jack, see your local electronics shop about an attenuating cable or other adapter that will reduce the output before it goes into the mic jack.

Watch your volume

Watching your volume should actually be the first ten rules on this list. It can't be emphasized too much. Your sound input level must be carefully controlled. If not, one of two things will happen: The recording will be soft and very noisy, or it will be loud and distorted. You need to find a happy medium. We'll talk about that more in the next section.

Avoid using a microphone directly

There are two reasons to avoid plugging a microphone directly into a sound card. First, it is very difficult to control recording consistency. It is much better to do several takes on tape and then record the best one directly from the tape recorder's output. This makes it easier to find a good clip, control the loudness, and avoid fumbling with the mike while you're trying to use the keyboard or mouse. The second reason is that it gives you the opportunity to plug the tape recorder into the sound card's line input. This is important because it avoids the card's microphone amplification circuitry. In an electrically noisy environment like the inside of a computer, you want to avoid as much amplification as possible because the noise gets amplified right along with your sound signal. If you frequently need to use a microphone live, and have a line level input jack available, consider getting a line level (preamplified) microphone at your local electronics shop or music store.

Be patient

It often takes time and many attempts to get a recording just right. Once you get an optimal setup and have had some practice, that time and experimentation can usually be avoided and you can get right down to business. Just remember that professional recording engineers spend years learning their business, so be prepared to invest some time in learning and practice.

RECORDING SESSION IN PROGRESS

Now it's your turn to try your hand at recording. If you haven't used Blaster Master yet, you might want to go back to Chapter 2 and review some of the basics of using the program. Make sure you're in the \SEP\BMSTR directory and then type BMASTER to run the program. On the initial file selection screen, click on Record to go to Blaster Master's recording screen shown in Figure 3-1.

Checking Levels

Before doing anything else, click on the Scope button. This will bring up a real-time sound wave display very similar to the Audio Scope program in Chapter 1. The main thing to be concerned with here is how high the peaks of

Figure 3-1 Blaster Master's recording screen
(Sound Blaster Pro configuration)

the waveform get. If you have something in mind to record—a musical clip
from a tape, or just microphone input—try it now. Your goal is to keep the
waveform as wide vertically as possible so that it is almost, but not quite,
reaching the top and bottom of the display. Be certain that the tops of the
waves don't get squared off. Figure 3-2 shows the same input signal at three
different levels: a, just right, b, too soft, and c, too loud.

Notice that even when you're not making any sound, there is some activity
on the display—that's background noise. It can be caused by sounds nearby,
such as the computer's fan, or TV in the next room. Even if the room is completely silent, all electronic circuits contain low, but measurable, levels of random electrical activity. These circuits also pick up signals from other
components in your computer, much like radio receivers. If your input is too
soft, two things happen. First, your sound will not be loud enough to cover up
the background noise. Because the sound was soft, you'll have to crank up
your speakers on playback to hear it. As you do that, the noise (which was
recorded along with your basic sound) will be amplified also. Second, recall
what we said in Chapter 1 about the number of bits of sampling resolution
and signal to noise ratio. That was a different kind of noise; it was added by
the step-like squaring off of the signal during sampling. The lower the input
level, the smaller the numbers need to be to record the sampled signal. Smaller
numbers effectively mean a smaller number of useful bits, and therefore a
lower signal to noise ratio caused by the sampling process itself. In other
words, you're in double trouble: the background noise is a more significant
part of the signal, and sampling noise becomes much more prominent. How

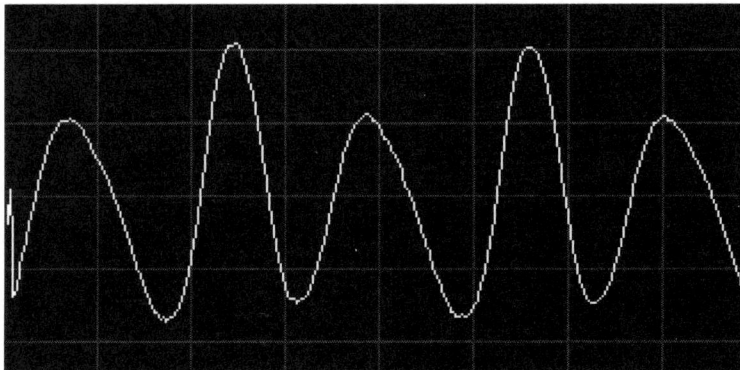

(a) just right

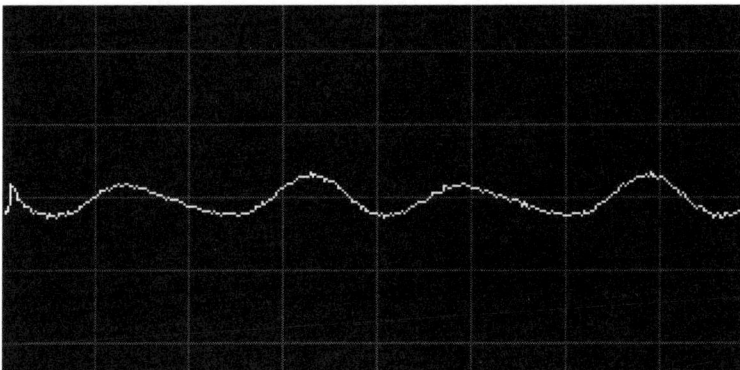

(b) too soft

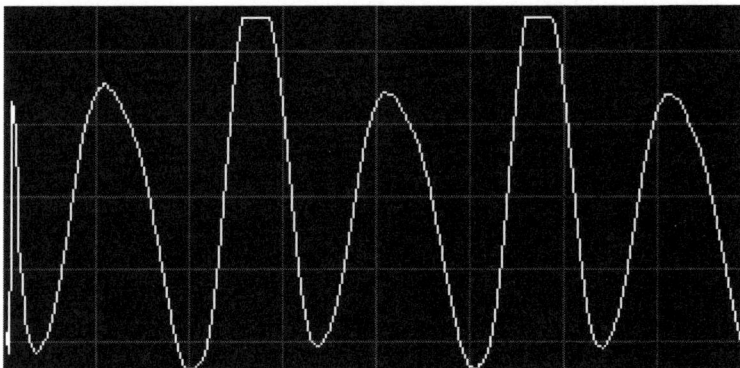

(c) too loud

Figure 3-2 Paying attention to recording levels can avoid noise and distortion

do you cure this? Simply keep the input volume levels as high as possible to reduce the effects of these two noise sources.

What about a signal that's too loud? This is actually a much worse problem than noise because the signal can be completely destroyed. Notice how the peaks get chopped off the signal that's too loud in Figure 3-2c. Do those peaks just dissipate as heat and contribute to global warming? Well, maybe they do, but the important thing is that what you see is what's being recorded. And what you see is a very different waveform than what's shown in Figure 3-2a. Remember that every sound wave can be produced by adding a series of simple, pure (sine) waves. It takes some pretty creative addition of waves to come up with something rounded with a flat top. And that comes in the form of lots of rogue frequencies that do anything but enhance the sound. This is distortion, and depending on how much of it there is, you may hear anything from occasional popping, to a recording that is completely unrecognizable. So keep those peaks from hitting!

The Actual Recording

After all this buildup, you'll probably find the recording process itself anticlimactic. If you're still looking at the Scope display, press (ESC) to return to the recording screen. Type in the name of a file you want to record into, for example, TAKE1.VOC. Check the sampling rate (number of samples per second to record) and see that it makes sense for the sound card you're using. For older Sound Blasters, 12,000 or 13,000 is a reasonable limit; newer units can go to 22,000 and beyond. For now, don't get too carried away; pick a conservative number, say, 11,000. Then get your sound source ready and click Record to start the process. When you're done, press (ESC).

That's all there is to it! After the recording completes, you're placed on the old familiar editing screen with your newly recorded waveform visible. At this point, you can perform any of the types of processing discussed in Chapter 2; the sound is yours to do with as you please.

Note: The shareware version of Blaster Master will only edit up to 25 seconds of sound.

You might want to try experimenting with a number of different sampling rates to get an idea of how they sound on your system, and to determine the minimum rate that you find acceptable. Keep in mind that if you plan to ulti-

mately use your recording with Windows applications, the three sampling rates that are typically supported are 44 kHz, 22 kHz, and 11 kHz. Use the Record option on the File pull-down menu to begin a new recording.

HELP! MY DISK IS FULL!

We have one last recording issue to worry about: audio files are BIG. This is not an overstatement. In fact, they can be downright HUGE. If you have a sound card capable of recording stereo at 16-bit resolution using a sampling rate of 44.1 kHz, one minute of sound will take over 10 megabytes! Figure 3-3 shows how much space that one minute of sound will take using several bit resolutions and sampling rates.

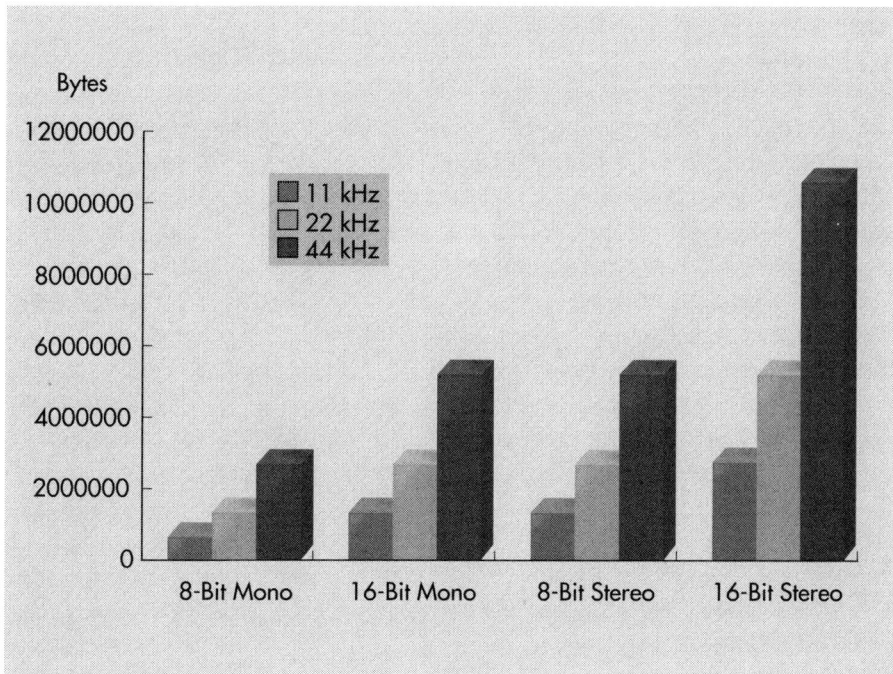

Figure 3-3 File sizes required for one minute of sound using different sampling rates and resolutions

To estimate the size of a file, multiply the sampling rate by the number of seconds you want to record. If you are recording using 16 bits, double that number. If you are recording in stereo, double it again.

So how do we solve this problem? One way is to look critically at how good the recording quality needs to be. If you are recording a hit track for a CD, certainly pull out all the stops. But if you're recording voice, you can get away with very modest settings for sample rate and resolution. Recall our discussion in Chapter 1 about sampling rate versus frequency content of the recorded material. If you can estimate the highest frequency contained in the material, double that number and add a little slop to get a reasonable sampling rate. To capture speech, which has very little frequency content beyond 4 to 5 kHz, a sampling rate of 11 kHz will be more than adequate; you'll find that even 6 kHz may give good enough results. For music, you'll want to hear higher frequencies, and the difference will be especially obvious in percussion sounds. Many people don't hear an appreciable improvement in most source material when using more than 22 kHz, so that's a reasonable upper limit for many recordings.

When do you need stereo, and when should you use 16 bits? Let your ears be your guide. Only a very few applications need stereo at all, so why double the space? Go with mono when you can. Listen to the difference between 8 and 16 bits. The big advantage of 16 bits is that it gives you much quieter recordings (less noise). If you don't find the extra noise objectionable, use 8 bits. In any case, try to balance resolution and sampling rate. For example, don't do 8-bit recording at 44.1 kHz, or 16-bit recording at 6 kHz. The strengths of one will not make up for the weaknesses of the other.

What about compression? This is a thorny issue. If you've tried using some of the popular data compression packages with audio files, chances are you've found that they usually work very poorly, and may actually increase the size of the file. This is because so-called lossless compression of audio (where no information is lost) is very difficult, due to the randomness in the sound waves. Text compresses well because it's very predictable; not so with audio. All of the sound files on the accompanying disks were compressed using lossless methods, but as you may have noticed, the expansion process is slow in some cases. Lossy compression is more commonly used for audio, as it trades off sound accuracy for increased speed and greater size reduction. Depending on the intended uses, it can be very effective, or it can be dreadful. Because we needed to maintain high accuracy for some of the included sound files, especially the processed 3-D samples, we chose a slower, lossless approach.

Blaster Master has the ability to pack, or do lossy compression, on .VOC files. You can try this out by pressing the Pack button on the editing display. It gives you three options: 4 Bit (2 samples per byte), 2.6 Bit (3 samples per byte), and 2 Bit (4 samples per byte). All of these are lossy because some data must be thrown out in the process. Once a file is packed, it can be restored to the original format, but never the original quality. Try loading STEP1.VOC and see how the different packing options affect it. As sound cards gain more processing power and software gets more sophisticated, expect to see both hardware and software compression techniques that help overcome this vexing problem of large audio files.

CONCLUSION

When you put together all the little things that can go wrong, it may seem amazing that we can do recording on personal computers at all. Fortunately, the quality of sound cards keeps improving, and sound software is getting smarter every day. With capable assistants like that, it's becoming an easier process. But there are always trade-offs, and only you can make the final decisions. Do you absolutely need a bigger disk to capture all those high frequencies, or would you rather spend the money on a vacation instead? Are 8 bits enough to prepare those home video narrations, or should you buy a 16-bit card? These aren't easy questions. Being realistic about your sound quality needs and understanding what the trade-offs are can help you make more intelligent decisions. At this point, you should have enough background to start attacking those problems and come up with workable compromises.

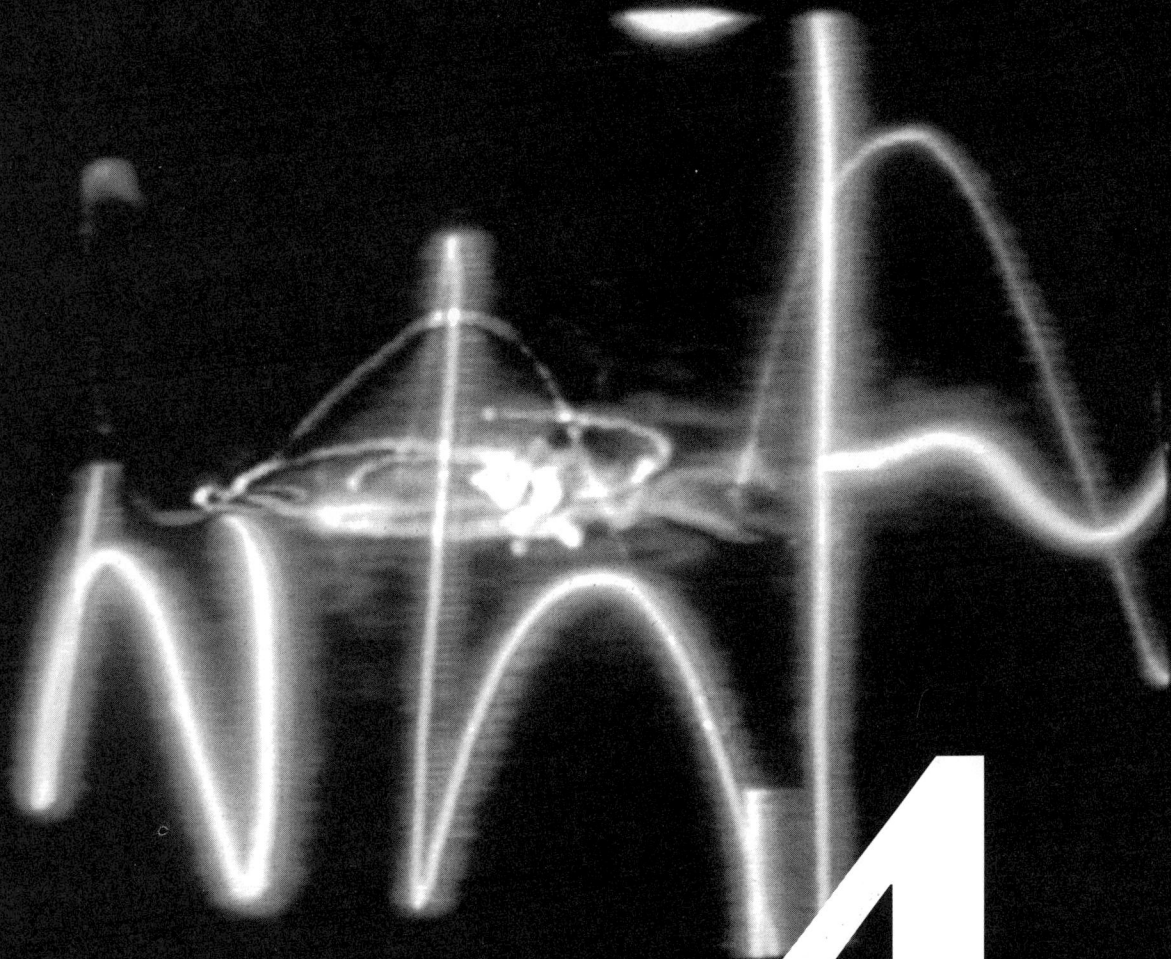

4

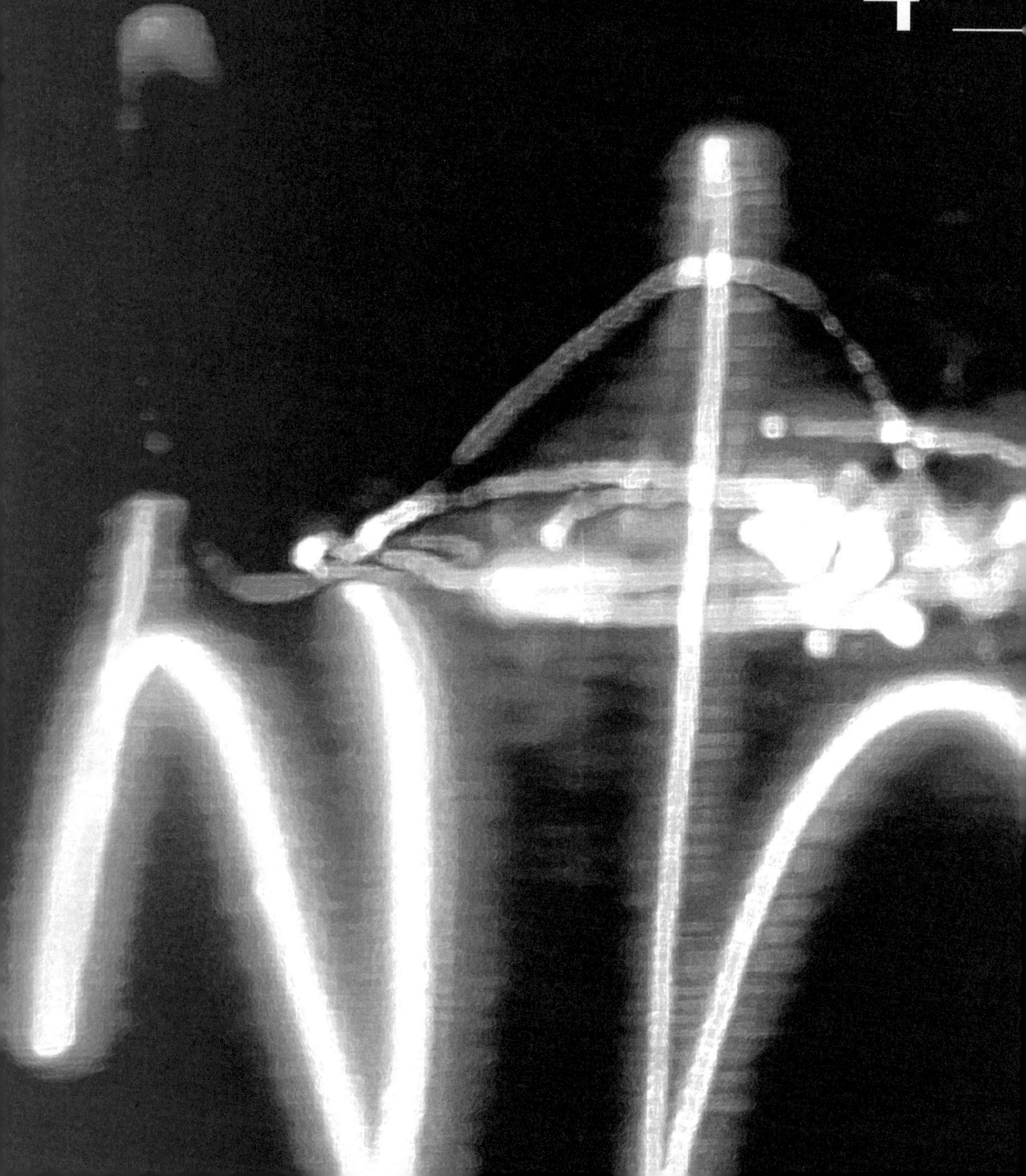

4

Speech

Sci-fi buffs have always known that it was just a matter of time before we would be communicating with our machines through spoken words. Stanley Kubrick's talking computer HAL in "2001: A Space Odyssey" first captured the imagination of the public at large, showing them an ominous image of technology taking control. What made the scenario most frightening was the humanizing effect of speech on an otherwise uninteresting piece of hardware. The addition of that simple quality vividly brought home the power of that most natural form of human communication. In this chapter, we'll look at some of the challenges of getting computers to speak and listen. After a brief overview of the basics of speech, along with some voice experiments, we'll have some fun with a simple voice-activated game. Maybe your computer will be more obedient than HAL.

SPEAKING

Even though small children can speak easily (too easily, some might argue), speech is an extremely complex process. A lot is already known about it, but if you've listened to the speech synthesis programs that come with most sound cards, you know we have a lot further to go in our understanding. Although

we can get close, and sometimes skirt the issue, natural-sounding speech generated by computers is not an easy goal.

Voice Response Systems

At present, the most reliable way to get a computer to speak is to play back audio clips of a real person speaking. If you've dialed a number equipped with a voice response system, such as a bank-by-phone service, you know this is a very reasonable approach. Such systems use a small set of recorded words and phrases that they can put together as necessary to form complete sentences (something like what we did in Chapter 2 when we digitally rearranged some words). There are two problems with these systems: They sound unnaturally choppy, and the restricted vocabulary limits their flexibility. But that's okay if you just need your account balance.

The choppiness in voice response systems is due to the fact that words spoken alone sound very different than spoken in a phrase. Words tend to blend together in real speech, as you no doubt found out the hard way if you've ever studied a foreign language. No amount of book study can prepare you for picking out newly learned words from a sentence in a foreign tongue.

Speech Generation

Creating speech out of the blue is by no means an easy task. At first glance, you might think you can just record a set of sounds corresponding to each letter in the alphabet, and you've got it made. Sounds good, but just as words run together in a sentence, so do sounds within a word. And there is no simple match between letters and sounds. English speech, for example, uses about 42 different sounds to make up words; these sounds are called phonemes. Look in any dictionary and you'll see a phonetic spelling for each word showing the phonemes that make it up. To see the problem, take the letter "s" in the following words: treasure, sure, and survey. The "sur" part is the same, but the "s" sound is distinctly different in each. So our first obstacle is just trying to determine which phonemes correspond to which parts of the word.

Assuming we get as far as figuring out the phonemes, things just get more complicated. We need to know how the different phonemes blend when placed next to each other, how they are reduced or slurred over in different words, where the accents fall on the word, the gender of the speaker, inflection at the ends of sentences, which words sound differently depending on

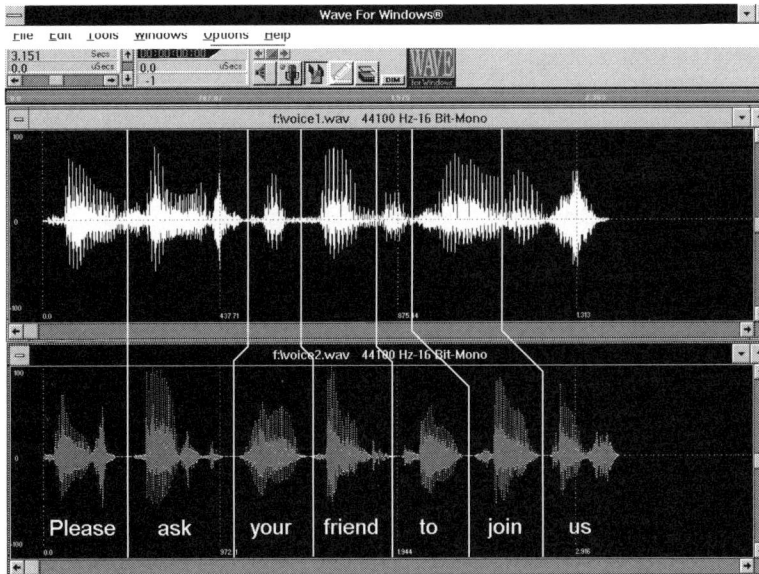

Figure 4-1 Words blended together in sentences sound very different than when spoken separately

their use in the sentence ("lead," for example), and so on. Because there are so many variations in the sounds when they are combined, we really can't rely on recorded phonemes, so we have to use some sort of sound generator to give us the qualities we need, when we need them. As you'll see in the next section, even the individual speech sounds themselves are very complex, so that's yet another hurdle. This is not a weekend project!

The top part of Figure 4-1 shows the audio waveform corresponding to the sentence "Please ask your friend to join us." Compare this to the same words spoken individually on the bottom. It's difficult to see where some of the words in the continuous version begin and end. Say the sentence out loud, speaking slowly and dragging out the sounds; try to hear how the words blend from one to the next. Unless we really concentrate, we don't even realize that there are such drastic variations in the words when we're speaking. Notice, for example, how the "z" sound at the end of "Please" blends into "ask," almost as if saying "plee-zask." A similar effect occurs between the other pairs of words. Also notice how the words "your" and "to" get reduced in continuous speech. These blendings and mutations may be easy for us to cope with, but they pose difficult problems in computer speech generation and recognition.

LISTENING

Although speech production is a complicated process by itself, the receiving end—hearing and understanding spoken words—is even more complex. To help us get a better idea of how computers can recognize words, we'll be using tools in the \SEP\SOUND directory. Change to that directory, and if you haven't already done so in Chapter 1, run the SNDSETUP program to make sure the other programs can correctly access your sound card. You'll also need a microphone attached to your sound card because you will be doing most of the talking.

Frequency Analysis

Let's look at some sounds to see what kinds of problems they may pose for a computer, and what properties we can see that might help. First, run Craig Walsh's MicFFT program to look at the frequency makeup of various word sounds. Type MF to start it, and press the (SPACEBAR) to begin processing. Try hissing first (hold the "s" sound at the beginning of the word "say"). Notice that the frequencies of that sound are spread out evenly, with a small buildup at the lower frequencies (on the left). Now try the "sh" from "show"; you should see a rise in the higher frequencies (on the right). In both cases, what we have is mostly random noise caused by the flow of air past the teeth, modified by the shape of the lips and mouth. These are called unvoiced sounds.

Another type of sound is a plosive, which is basically a burst (or explosion) of air caused by closing and then releasing part of the vocal tract. The letter "p" is a good example. Because these are short sounds, they probably won't show up very well in MicFFT, so let's move along.

The vowels (a, e, i, o, u) are all good examples of voiced sounds. To be voiced, a sound must have some component caused by the vibration of the vocal chords. Try saying "ahhhhh," and notice some very strong frequency peaks with much less random noise. Try the other vowels and notice the different sets of peaks. Then try to say an extended "zh" sound like the "s" in "treasure." This is a combination of a voiced and unvoiced sound. It's like the "sh" sound, but it vibrates like a vowel.

Now try one more experiment. Make any vowel sound, hold it, and at the same time, raise or lower your pitch as if you were singing. Even though the frequency peaks shift around, they retain much of their basic shape. Try a dif-

ferent vowel—it'll behave the same way, though with different peaks. These strong peaks, called formants, stay relatively uniform and can be used to help distinguish between various vowels and other voiced sounds.

Because of the different frequency makeup of the sounds in speech, it is possible to categorize and identify them using frequency-based analysis techniques such as the Fast Fourier Transform used in MicFFT. If you have a slower machine, you can immediately see a problem with that approach: it takes a long time to do the calculations, certainly too long for real-time speech analysis. If you don't have the time, you can resort to specialized hardware to help out. This is exactly what some of the newer sound boards are doing, incorporating a DSP, or digital signal processor, to speed up this kind of processing.

Other Clues

So what do you do if you don't have a really fast machine or special hardware to do speech recognition? No, you're not left out in the cold. There are many ways to look at speech and extract useful information. Run the Word Scope program in the \SEP\SOUND directory by typing WSCOPE. This is a close relative of the Audio Scope program from Chapter 1. The difference is that Word Scope captures short sounds (up to about 1.5 seconds) and graphs some useful information about them. Try not to jostle the microphone too much while using it because the program will capture each distinct sound that's loud enough to trigger it.

Word Scope demonstrates two very simple types of information that we can extract from a spoken word without resorting to heavy computing. Say the word "yes" and look at the graph it makes, shown in Figure 4-2. The upper line (blue on your screen) is a measure of the energy in the word over time, and comes from simple calculations on the sampled data. The lower line (red on your screen) shows zero-crossings—a sort of cheap frequency measure. It comes from counting the number of times the waveform switches back and forth, and gives an indication of the high frequency content of the signal.

What does it all mean? The upper energy line (blue) gives some clues to the type of sound. For example, voiced sounds have much higher energy than unvoiced ones, and show as higher points on the graph. Higher frequency components, especially in noisier sound sections, show up as a rise in the lower (red) zero-crossings line. But in some ways, it doesn't even matter what the graphs mean. What is important is that for a given word, the graph will

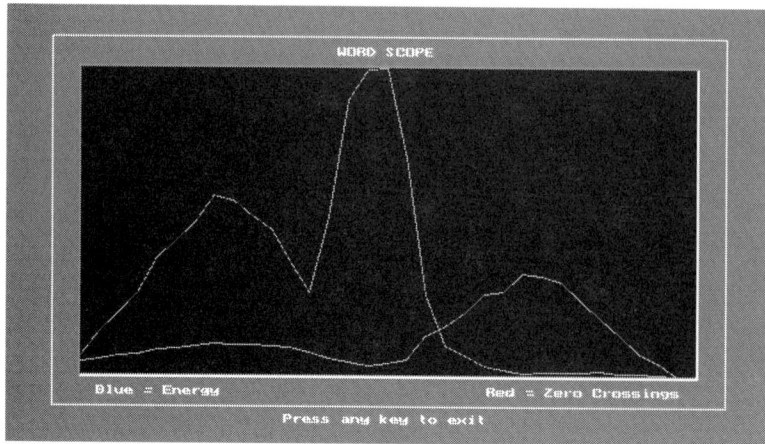

Figure 4-2 Word Scope plot showing energy and frequency content of the word "Yes"

always look pretty much the same. Say "yes" several times, trying to be as clear and uniform as you can each time; they should all produce the same rough shapes. Now try the word "no" (see Figure 4-3). Very different, isn't it? Try other words and see if you can identify the sections of sound in each word by their appearance on the display.

Simply by storing the information in these graphs for a set of words, it's possible to match newly spoken words with the old ones and get a reasonable (not great, but acceptable) recognition rate. If the words you speak don't look

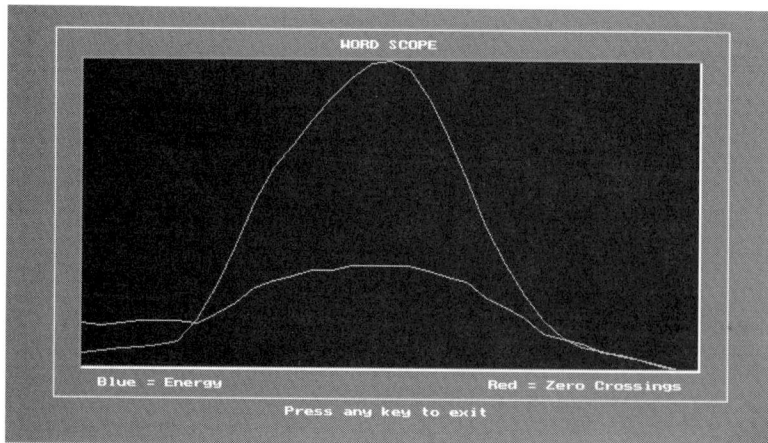

Figure 4-3 Word Scope plot of the word "No"

very similar on the Word Scope display, try practicing for a while. Saying words consistently is a necessary skill to succeed in the demo game in the following section.

SPEECH RECOGNITION

A number of different application areas employ the analysis of spoken words. On the cloak-and-dagger end of the spectrum, speaker verification is a hot topic, where the goal is to identify a speaker as the correct person. A person's voice is as unique as a fingerprint, but since it's always changing slightly, it's more of a challenge to match accurately. In this section, we'll be concerned with speech recognition, rather than speaker recognition. Speech recognition involves identifying spoken words so they can be used to control computers and provide data input.

Classifications

There are several different classes of speech recognition systems: some are easier to build than others. Speaker-independent recognition is a difficult process because of the enormous variety in people's voices. Speaker-dependent processing is much easier because the system only has to be trained to recognize a single person or a small group of people. Because of the way words flow together, continuous speech processing requires special care to separate the words. Isolated speech recognition, on the other hand, is much simpler. The following demo combines the two simplest types: speaker-dependent and isolated speech recognition.

The Game

Enough theory, let's get down to business. In the \SEP\SOUND directory, type VDEMO to start up the voice command game. It doesn't really have a name, but if you like, you can call it "Attack of the Killer Triangles." You have sentry posts down the left and little triangular attackers moving in from the right. Your job is to place and train sentries to fend off the attackers. Each sentry is a word or short phrase that you type in. These sentries don't pay much attention, so you need to wake them up by—you guessed it—shouting their names! Well,

you don't really have to shout, a nice clear voice command will do. When you get a sentry's attention, it puts up a blockade that prevents any attacker from getting through. All the sentries share the same blockade, so you have to keep shuttling it around to ward off the invading...whatever they are.

Before the game can start (unless you want to suffer utter defeat), you need to train the sentries to recognize their names. First type a word or short phrase into each sentry position. Use the arrow keys or mouse to select them. The more unique the words you pick, the better your chances for recognition. Try names of family and friends, for example (you might have some you don't want to train so well). It doesn't matter what you pick, as long as you can say it in about a second and a half. Avoid short, similar sounding words; single letters are a bad choice. Figure 4-4 shows the initial screen layout with the first phrase position selected.

Now to train the troops. Move to each one in turn and press F2 to begin training. You will be asked to say the word or phrase several times so that an average can be taken. Speak loudly and clearly; uniformity is the key. If you think you'll get excited in the heat of battle, don't forget that your inflections might change. Shouting at a sentry after training it in a mellow voice won't get you very far.

You can test the training at any point by saying a sentry's name. A little blue blockade will appear to the right of the sentry when it hears you. If some sentries don't respond very well, try retraining just the ones with problems. If that doesn't help, try more recognizable words. When you feel you have a reasonably competent outfit, you can press F7 to begin the game.

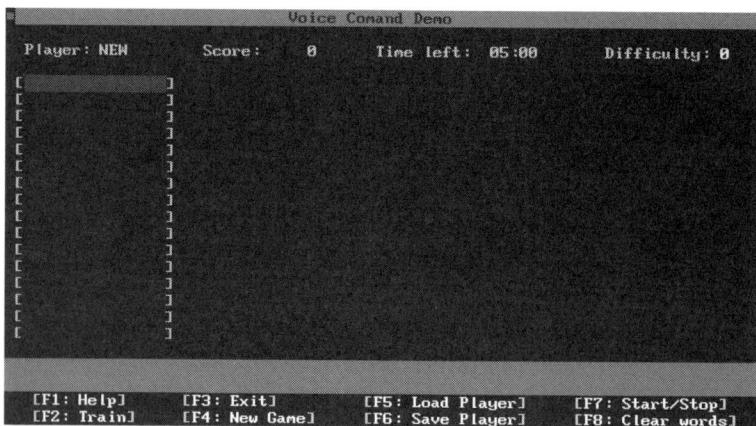

Figure 4-4 Voice recognition game—initial screen layout

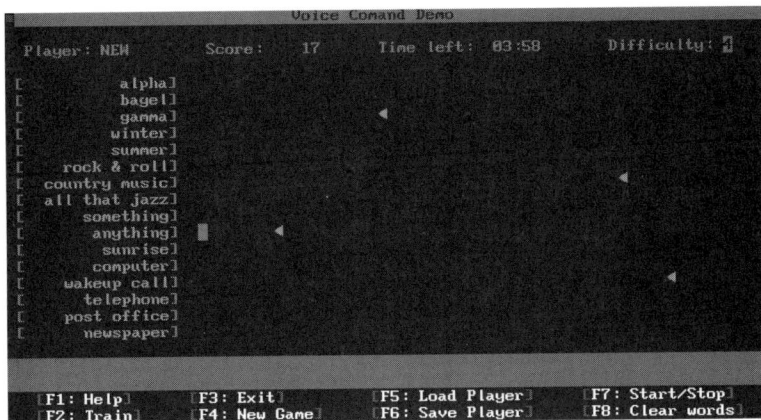

Figure 4-5 Voice recognition game with sentries trained and attackers approaching

You score each time a sentry blocks an attacker. Note that depending on the amount of time it takes to process commands, you may see some slow-down in the attackers while speaking. You get five minutes of playing time to start. You'll also get more time as you successfully gather points. When time runs out, the game is over. You can set the intensity of play to higher levels by changing the difficulty factor in the upper-right corner—0 is easiest, 9 is most frantic. That's all there is to it, except for one annoying little catch: If a sentry gets hit by an attacker, it gets hurt. In particular, it starts to lose its memory and is less likely to recognize its name. This means you may have to retrain a sentry after some hits. You can suspend play to retrain by pressing (F7) (but a real general wouldn't).

Figure 4-5 shows the game display with the sentries already trained and play in progress. If you want to play the game with friends, each of you will need your own set of command phrases. This is a speaker-dependent recognizer, so it is unlikely that another person would be able to use your commands. To save yours, press (F5) and type a file name (no extension needed) to write your commands and the recognition information to disk. Then press (F8) to clear the current list so your friend can start. To recall your commands later for a new game, press (F6) and type your file name.

Have fun! Remember, use clear and consistent speech. If you're having trouble, go back and try the Word Scope program again to see why your words may be varying, and practice getting a uniform appearance. This program uses a very simple-minded recognizing scheme, without much room for

53

error. It wouldn't be useful for getting any real work done, but doesn't do a bad job of simulating a sleepy sentry.

Windows users can try out a demo of a much more sophisticated voice recognition system, called IN3, in Chapter 10. IN3 shows you how voice commands can add significantly to your productivity. And it hardly ever goes to sleep!

CONCLUSION

There are many challenges involved in computer speech generation and recognition. Because of this, the whole area is lagging well behind other computer sound applications. Both speech input and output are here today, but your mileage may vary. Highly accurate recognition systems can be had—for a price. Inexpensive systems have a lot of drawbacks, and none can be used in full dictation applications; but for simple word control, the future is now.

Computers that speak and respond to spoken words can bring us to new levels of effectiveness in using them. You may be put off at first by the notion of holding a conversation with a machine; you may even be offended by the idea of your computer becoming too personal. Whatever your feelings, you'll soon find that, at the very least, it's a whole lot of fun. Sure, your family, friends, and coworkers may look at you strangely as you happily chat with your machine, but they'll soon become accustomed to it. Beware: It is addicting, and no matter how silly it might look now, that's nothing compared to how it will look when you start talking to computers that are not voice capable!

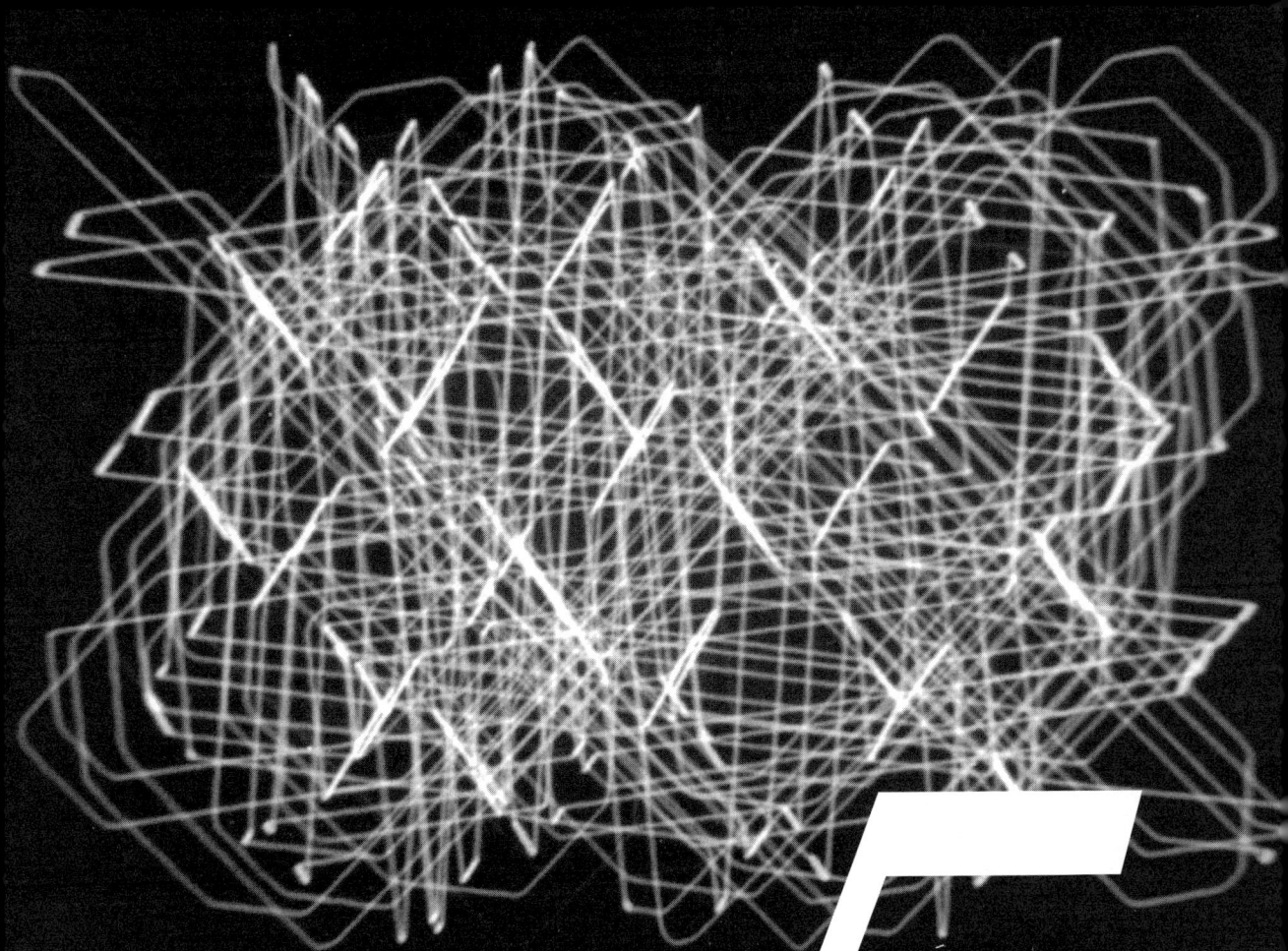

5

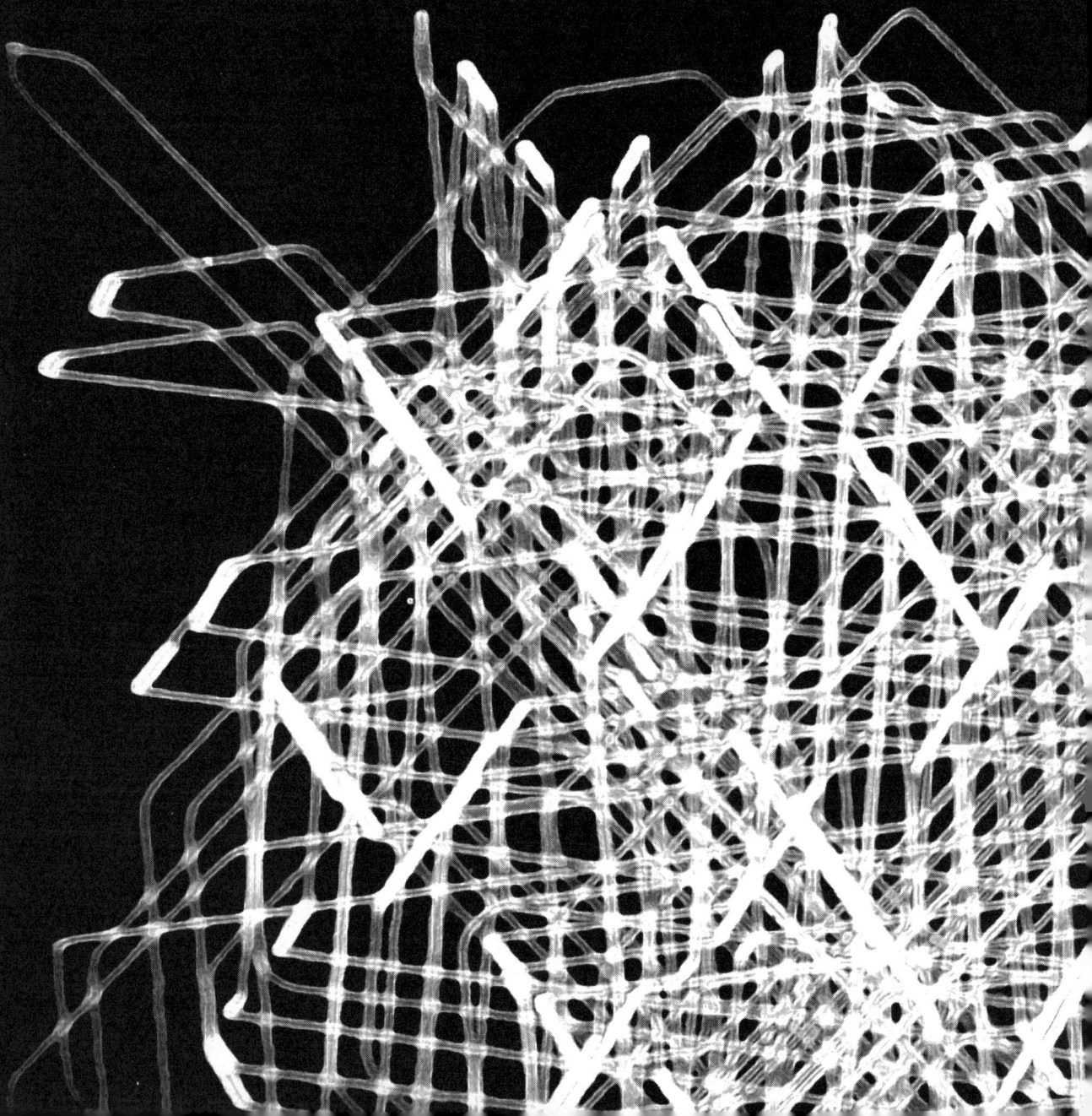

Three-Dimensional Sound

If you've ever seen a 3-D movie, you know how startling the effect can be when an object jumps out of the screen at you. You may have even raised your hands to protect yourself. Now imagine hearing sounds from your stereo speakers that are so realistic, you find yourself looking all around the room, following them. An arrow flies by your head and you duck. A dog barks at you from under the coffee table and you jump. You know there's nothing there, but you can't help yourself, the imagery is so real.

A new crop of audio products is trying to break with the traditions of stereo recording and place you in the middle of the action. In this chapter, you'll learn how we are able to so accurately hear the position of sounds, and find out how some companies are making products that fool your ears into "seeing" sounds anywhere a producer wants you to. One such company is QSound, and we'll get a taste of how their technology works by listening to some short sound clips produced using their patented process.

WHERE IS THAT SOUND COMING FROM?

You've probably asked the question, "Where is that sound coming from?" many times. Hearing is not our most precise sense for examining the environment, but if someone drops a glass behind you, you know pretty well what happened and where. Those times when we hear a sound and can't quite pinpoint it are actually rare compared to the thousands of times a day we use hearing to localize some sound. Most of the time we don't even do it consciously; we're constantly evaluating sounds as part of our early warning system to tell when things are afoot.

When we hear a nearby sound, we usually know approximately where it is on a 360-degree circle around us, how high (or low) it is, and how far away it is. Just as our two eyes give us depth perception, so do our two ears work together to perceive locations of sounds. It might surprise you to learn, however, that even with only one ear, a person can still learn to perceive direction fairly accurately. There are many factors at work here, which should be no surprise after going through the earlier material in this book.

What are some of the things that let us pick out sound locations? The first, and most obvious clue comes from the intensity of the sound reaching each ear. Something to the left will usually sound louder in the left ear. There's kind of a sonic shadow that keeps the right ear from hearing as much. This is only a rough clue, however. For certain frequencies (up to around 800 Hz), another clue is the lag in time between the sound reaching both ears (sound isn't quite like light, it does flow around objects). Just the very slight delay—measured in millionths of a second—between when sound hits the first ear and the second, is enough to help identify its location (see Figure 5-1). Human voices, plus many musical instruments, fall into the category of sounds that can be pinpointed in this manner. Very low frequency sounds, such as pulsating machine noises, are often impossible to locate; they may actually be the most common source of the "Where is that coming from?" question. Locating high frequencies depends on other factors.

Familiarity is one very important factor in determining distance. As sound travels through the air and past objects, it loses high frequency information and picks up echoes, so things in the distance tend to sound dulled. This is why thunder nearby cracks sharply, but rumbles in the distance. Not being familiar with a sound, however, we wouldn't know if it should be sharp or dull to begin with.

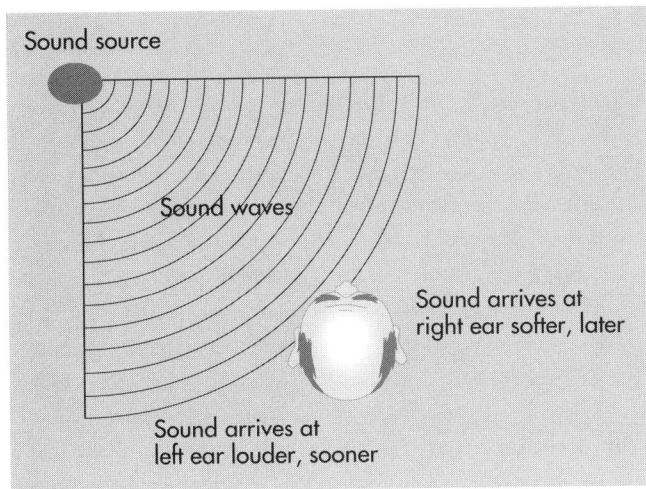

Figure 5-1 Sound waves arriving at our ears give directional information in the form of volume and timing differences

The shape of our outer ears also plays an important role, especially in identifying the vertical position of sounds and in determining whether the sounds are coming from in front or behind us. The ridges and folds in the outer ear cause very subtle blocking and reflection of sounds, modifying their frequency content ever so slightly, but enough for the brain to get a lot of directional information.

Reflections off objects, such as walls, cause timing and frequency variations that also contribute to sound location. In a story once relayed to the author, a certain blind college student was often seen walking down halls and across courtyards snapping his fingers. People often mistook him for a beatnik, as he happily snapped his fingers in time to some unheard music. He was actually using the snapping as a form of sonar, or echo location, to make his way around. In his case, the direction, intensity, and other properties of the echoes let him "see" his surroundings, often letting him pick up more detail than his sighted friends would notice.

We've only touched on some of the more important factors involved in directional hearing. There are many other subtle effects that contribute to this impressive ability. Suffice it to say that it is an extremely complex process, but one we handle quite easily.

MORE THAN STEREO

Our knowledge of how humans locate sounds is still quite limited. We do, however, know a lot more when it comes to creating sounds, and because of that, we can model real environments well enough to produce sounds that have specific effects, including placement at particular locations in space.

Some of you may remember the quadraphonic sound fad from the early 1970s, and the idea that using four speakers, two in front and two in back, would help reproduce the live listening environment. It met with some success, but it was never really that impressive, and besides, most people have enough trouble finding room for two speakers. That's not to shut the door on multi-speaker sound, however. Several new schemes are in use, or are being developed, that have much more promise for the future. You may have already heard the results of some of these sonic enhancements in movie theaters and on TV—Dolby Surround being one of them.

Some processes that try to add spaciousness and reproduce 3-D sound information involve working with already recorded material. A number of years ago, Carver Corporation introduced a consumer device that should win the award for the most impressive product name ever—the Sonic Holography Autocorrelator Preamp. If set up correctly, the results were also impressive, but a lot of the directional information in the sound had already been lost during the original recording process. To overcome this, newer schemes process the sound at the time the many separate tracks making up a recording are mixed to produce the final two tracks of stereo.

By applying what we already know about directional hearing, it is possible to build equipment based on frequency filtering and time shifting to adjust the sound for a more natural 3-D feel. Some methods require special decoding equipment to play back the sound to achieve a 3-D effect. Others, like QSound, which we'll look at next, require no special listening equipment beyond stereo speakers. Most of these systems have been targeted to the professional audio market for use in enhancing commercial stereo recordings, but the technology is now filtering down to the personal computer multimedia market and promises soon to give consumers real-time control over 3-D audio imaging.

QSound

QSound Limited, a subsidiary of Archer Communications based in Calgary, Alberta, got its start doing real-time audio processing for the 1988 Winter

Olympics. From those beginnings came a remarkable new way to listen to sound. The company's main product is QSound, a 3-D sound processing technology which they incorporate into their own QSystem hardware and license to other vendors. QSound has become quite the rage, already having been used on dozens of albums by stars such as Madonna, Sting, and Paula Abdul. It has also appeared in movies, TV, and radio commercials.

What makes QSound different from most other 3-D products is that it's not based on theoretical models of human hearing and acoustics, but on the listening experiences of real, live people. During the design of QSound, the company performed over half a million listening tests to identify the subtle differences in the hearing process that account for our ability to localize sounds. Taking that mass of experimental data, experienced engineers using computer-aided design software painstakingly matched filter designs to the observed results. The ultimate goal was a processing technique that would give the same results for new sounds. Those results are, in fact, breathtaking.

Normal stereo places sounds within a rather limited area between the speakers (see Figure 5-2a). Very often with stereo, you hear a sound, look at the speaker, and you know the sound is coming directly from that speaker. QSound, on the other hand, lets a sound be placed anywhere within a 180-degree semicircle around the listener, as shown in Figure 5-2b. It not only works to place the sound around the listener at ear level, but above and below as well. You no longer hear sound coming from a particular speaker, but instead, from anywhere else. This illusion can be quite alarming at first!

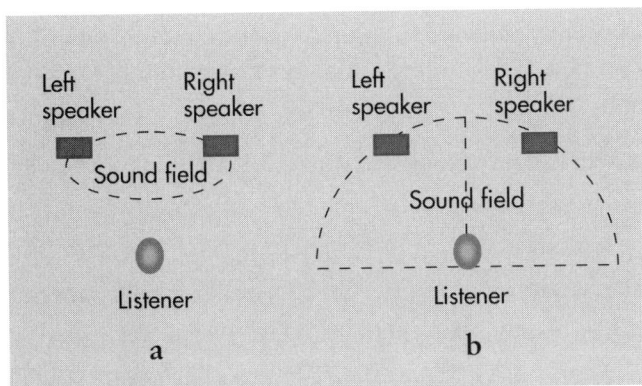

Figure 5-2 Apparent sound locations produced by (a) conventional stereo versus (b) QSound

Other than commercial recordings, one of the first big target markets for QSound is in computer and arcade games. QSound-processed sound tracks on disk and CD-ROM will add a new sense of realism to games, putting you right into the action. But soon, QSound's effects won't be limited to prerecorded material. Producing a professional multitrack recording requires huge amounts of processing power and hardware that cost many thousands of dollars. The QSound technology has been down-scaled, however, and can now be built right into consumer products for applications which are less demanding. Expect to see games where objects can be heard all around you, placed according to the natural flow of the game, and not according to some predetermined soundtrack.

Demo Setup

Thanks to the people at QSound and Sound Source Unlimited, we've included some sample 3-D audio clips. You can find these clips in the \SEP\QSOUND directory. Before trying them out, you'll need to make sure your stereo speakers are set up properly. Here are some important guidelines to follow in order to get the best QSound effect:

- Make sure the volume level of each speaker is the same.

- If you use any kind of bass/treble control or other equalization, it must be set the same for both speakers.

- The included sound samples are set up for typical multimedia computer speakers placed on either side of your monitor, so the optimal distance between speakers is 20 to 24 inches.

- Place the speakers at the same level vertically, and for best results, slightly below ear level.

- Arrange your listening area so that you and the speakers are at the corners of an equilateral triangle, with the speakers both pointing forward (see Figure 5-3). They may be angled in slightly.

- The speakers should be at least three feet away from any side walls to avoid interference from those surfaces.

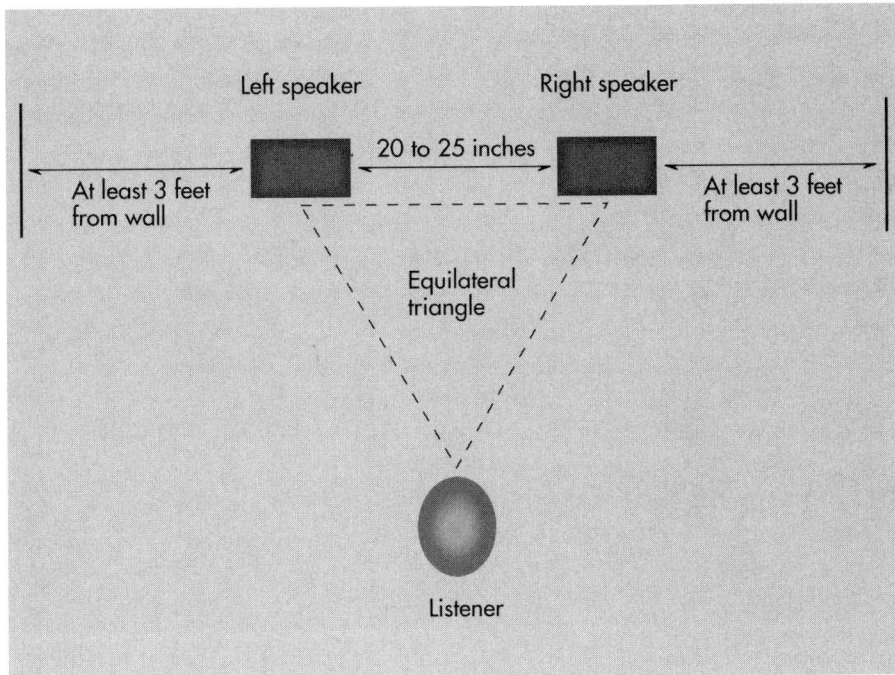

Figure 5-3 Optimum speaker placement and listener position for QSound

Although these samples will give you some 3-D feel using headphones, the effect will not be very great since the samples were generated for use with speakers. You may in fact hear sounds behind you, which may prove the 3-D point, but isn't quite what was intended.

The stereo sample files are in Windows' WAV format. In order to listen to them in DOS on a stereo Sound Blaster, you can use the Blaster Master program (refer to Chapter 2). Choose the Import function on the file selection screen to load the files and then play them as usual. If you have a Pro Audio Spectrum, you cannot use Blaster Master because the card is not Sound Blaster-stereo compatible; you must use the Play program that comes with the Pro Audio Spectrum (see your manual for details).

If you are using Windows, most standard WAV applications, such as the Media Player or Sound Recorder (discussed in Chapter 10), should be able to play the clips. Playing the sounds via the File Manager is probably easiest: Double-click on the File Manager icon in the Main program group; select the

\SEP\QSOUND directory; and finally, double-click on each QSound file to listen to it (the File Manager automatically runs the Media Player or Sound
Recorder to play .WAV files).

CONCLUSION

We hope you were able to hear the dramatic effects of QSound using just your
sound card and a pair of speakers. Right now, QSound is one of the leaders in
this area, but many other companies are hot on their trail with a new generation of multidimensional sound enhancement technology. Quadraphonics isn't
dead yet; some of the new schemes are pushing four channels as a way to get
even more realistic sounds. You should expect stereo enhancement to start
being used in virtually all commercial recordings in the not-too-distant future.
Three-dimentional sound features in computer games and sound cards are
starting to appear already. It's probably safe to assume that 3-D sound will
become commonplace long before 3-D video takes root in any big way.
There's a lot of interest, and a lot of promise.

For more information on QSound, contact them at:
QSound Ltd.
Archer Communications Inc.
2748—37 Avenue N.E.
Calgary, AB T1Y 5L3
Canada
(403) 291-2492

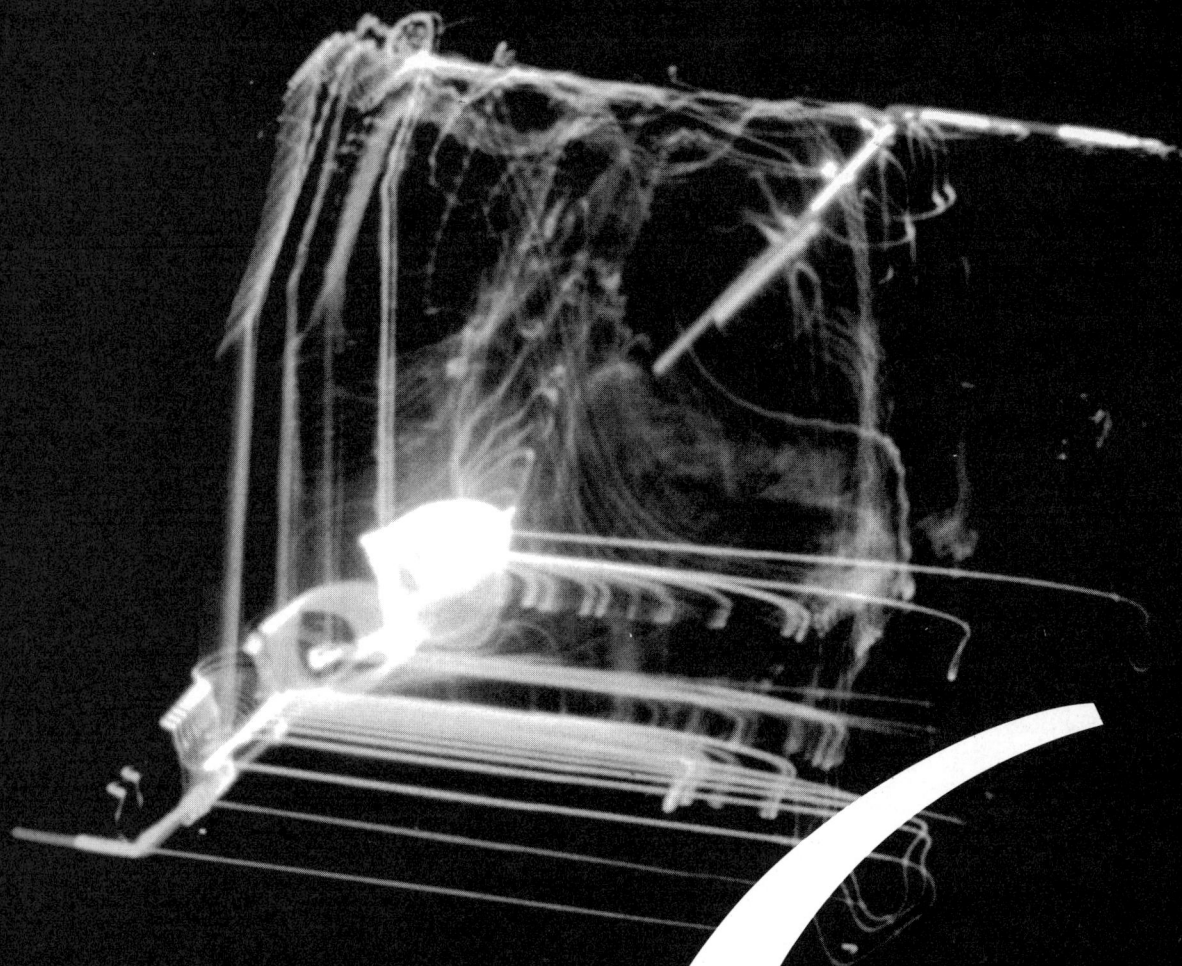

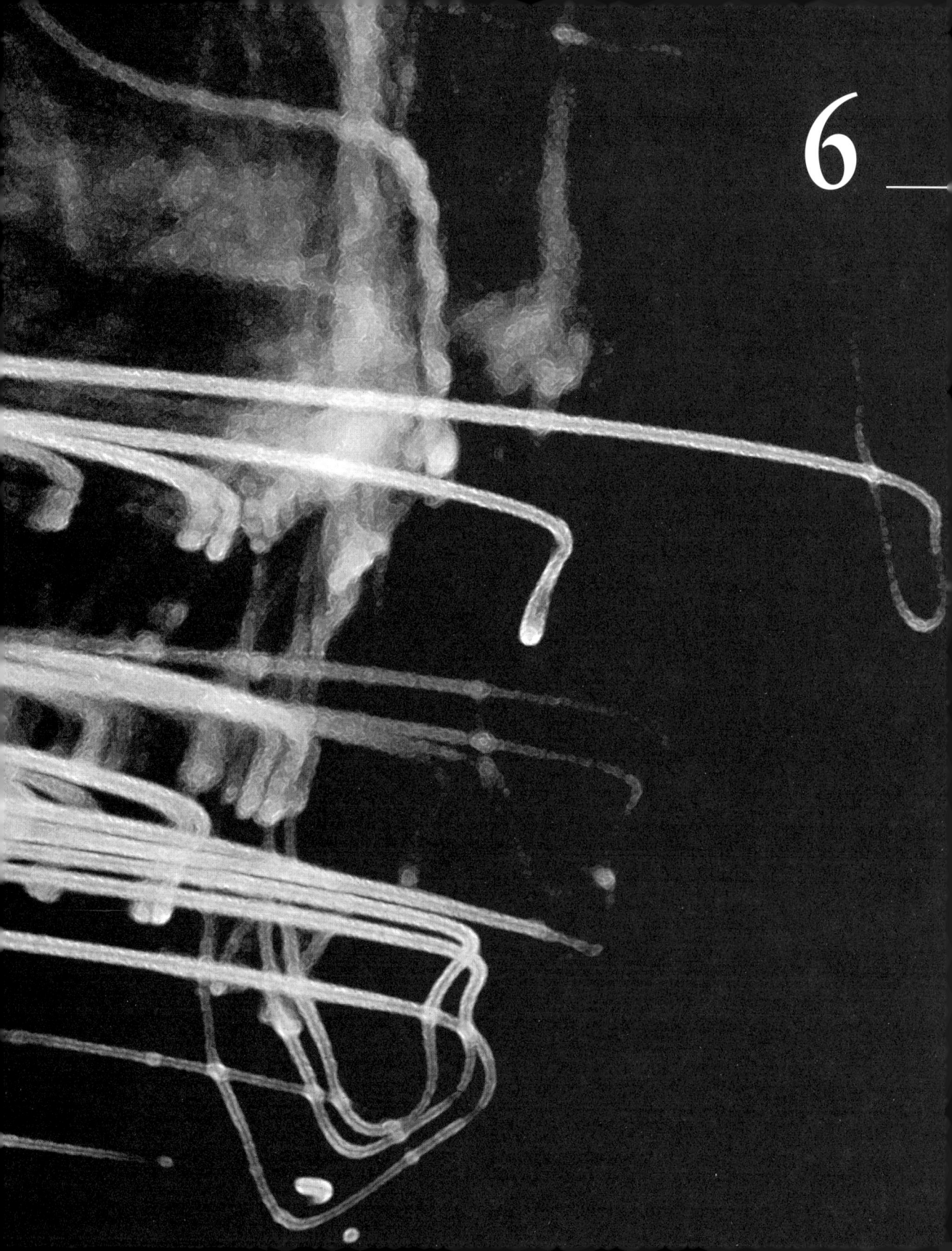

Sound Synthesis

So far, we've worked mostly with techniques that involve recordings of real sounds. Although we can cut and splice and change certain characteristics, we are very much limited by the original material. If a singer hits a slightly flat note, we can raise it using a little care, and no one will be the wiser. However, suppose we want a flute instead of a piano; there's no choice but to head back to the recording studio. And let's not forget all the space that digital recordings take up on disk, plus the difficulties of coping with noise and distortion. Fortunately, these limitations of digitized sound can be sidestepped by creating sounds on the fly using a powerful technique known as sound synthesis. This chapter provides the basic background material you need to effectively use sound synthesis, and then lets you jump in and get some hands-on experience sculpting sounds.

WHAT IS SYNTHESIS?

Sound synthesis can be defined simply as the creation of new sounds electronically. The word "new" is the key here. Of course, we've been creating sounds electronically all along, but they were all based on originally recorded material, possibly with some additional processing. Now we're going to be synthesizing, or creating from raw material, waveforms that never existed before.

Although we'll certainly be able to create sounds that are quite realistic, synthesized sounds can also go far beyond any that would ever exist in nature.

It has only been in recent years that falling prices for computer memory have let us make use of digitally sampled sounds at all, so there has been plenty of time for people to come up with ways of creating sounds without large investments in hardware. Serious sound synthesis research dates back several decades. Much of that work, combined with modern digital processing techniques, has yielded some astounding sound devices. They all offer strong advantages: minimal CPU overhead, much lower storage requirements, and the ability to command an infinite range of sounds.

The lines between synthesis and sound sample playback are becoming blurred, as many new products combine both techniques. In this chapter, however, we'll focus on synthesis alone, and in particular, the process called FM synthesis. Although many synthesis methods are in use, the vast majority of PC sound cards employ FM synthesis. These include the AdLib, Sound Blaster, Pro Audio Spectrum, and compatible cards. In fact, all of them use the same family of Yamaha sound chips to generate FM sound.

"FM" stands for frequency modulation, which is roughly the same process employed in FM radio. A complete understanding of frequency modulation requires in-depth mathematical analysis, but we can avoid much of the theory and concentrate on the practical aspects. You will see, for example, that even though a single FM sound may involve dozens of interrelated control settings, certain controls have much more impact on the sound than others. Concentrating on these, we can reduce the guesswork. Nevertheless, FM remains a complex subject and in order to make any headway, a certain amount of background material must be covered.

FM BASICS

You may have noticed the way a violin player's left hand often oscillates back and forth while pressing on the strings. This is not a bad habit the player picked up as a child to avoid hitting the notes squarely. The player is adding vibrato, a kind of pulsating change in the pitch of the note as the string's length and tension change. Vibrato is not a technical requirement of making violin tones, but we have become accustomed to this kind of embellishment, perhaps because it makes the tone more voicelike. But what does vibrato have to do with FM synthesis? Vibrato is one of the simplest forms of frequency

Higher frequency ← → Lower frequency ← → Higher frequency

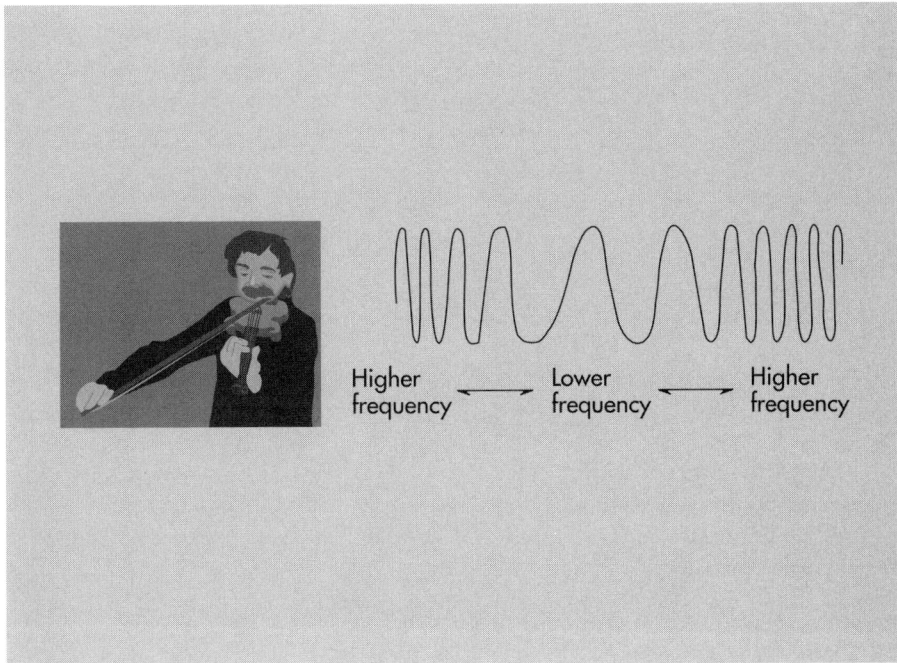

Figure 6-1 A violinist adding vibrato to a tone demonstrates a form of frequency modulation

modulation, and one that's easy for us to visualize; the pitch we hear modulates around the actual note being played. Note the way the sound wave alternates between a bunched-up higher frequency and a spread-out lower frequency in Figure 6-1.

The whistle blowing on a passing train also demonstrates a simple FM effect. As the train approaches, the sound waves are squeezed closer together because the train is catching up with the sound waves and we hear a higher pitch. As the train leaves, the sound waves spread out, causing us to hear a lower pitch (see Figure 6-2). This so-called Doppler effect, like vibrato, causes a single basic tone to change in pitch over time.

Unfortunately, these two examples are pretty much the extent to which our intuition can help us in understanding the concept of frequency modulation. As the modulating frequency increases, changes in the sound occur that are sometimes hard to describe in words: "It's fatter," "it has more texture," "there are more sounds in there." You get the idea—these are subjective impressions. You have to listen to the sounds to understand what's happening. The basic principle remains the same, however.

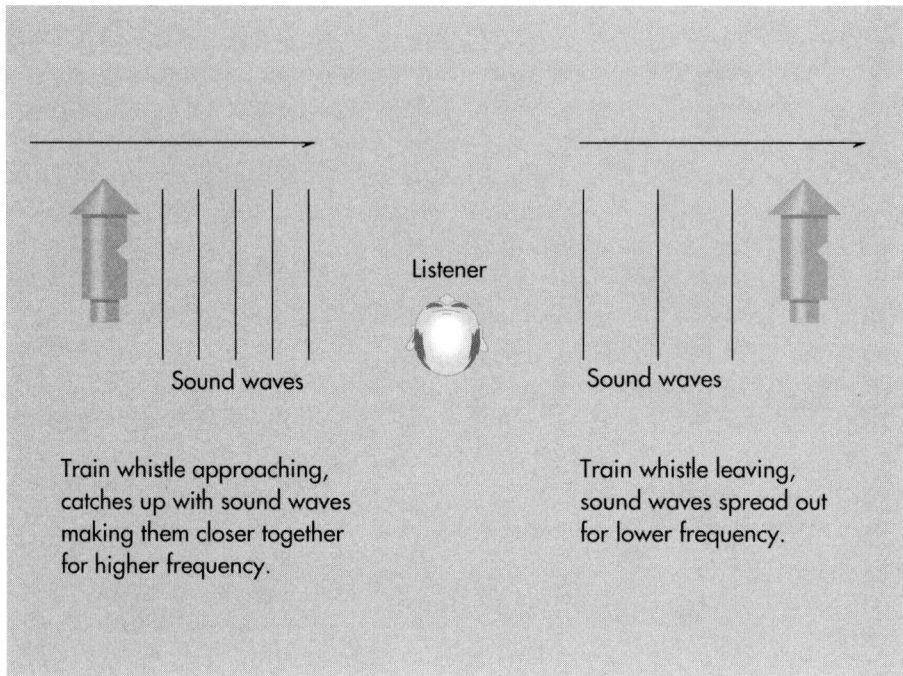

Figure 6-2 Doppler effect as a form of frequency modulation

In the simplest setup, FM synthesis requires two frequency generators, or oscillators (see Figure 6-3). The output of oscillator 2 is what we hear, and the output of oscillator 1 is used to modify the base frequency of oscillator 2. Keeping with the conventions of FM radio engineering, the frequency of oscillator 1 is called the modulating frequency, and the frequency of oscillator 2 is the carrier frequency.

In FM synthesis, the oscillators are usually called operators, and the two basic types are carriers and modulators. Each single sound produced by a synthesizer normally uses at least two operators, so a typical FM card needs lots of operators to handle the many notes that may be sounding at one time. Most popular cards contain 18 or 36 operators. Some cards also support combining more than two operators at a time in order to produce more complex sounds. But for now, let's concentrate on the very simple synthesizer in Figure 6-3. It lets us control the frequency and output levels for two operators, and produces a single sound. What does it sound like? Let's step through this slowly and listen to some examples. Change to the \SEP\FM directory and type FMSETUP to prepare the demos for use with your sound card.

Oscillator 1	Oscillator 2	
"Modulator"	"Carrier"	Output signal

The simple sweeping up and down of the modular waveform varies the frequency of the carrier.

Starting as a simple waveform itself, the carrier speeds up or slows down depending on the input from the modulator.

The resulting waveform appears compressed and expanded at higher and lower frequencies, respectively.

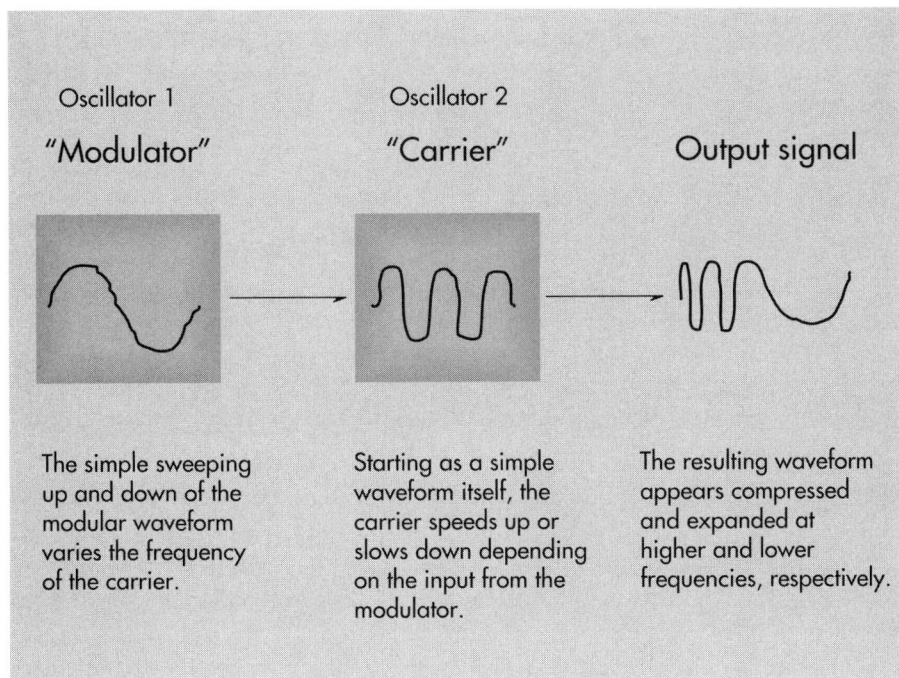

Figure 6-3 The components of a basic FM synthesizer

For the first example, start by turning off the modulator completely so that all we hear is the normal carrier output. It could be a simple sine wave, or something more complex, but it's typically not very interesting. Run sound example FM1 to get an idea (just type FM1 and press (ENTER)). In this case, what we hear is a dull old sine wave.

Now turn up the modulator output and set it to a low frequency. Run FM2 to hear the result—something a little more interesting. If you listen carefully, you'll hear a second, and maybe even a third tone mixed in with the original.

Next run FM3, where we turn up the modulator output to a medium level (remembering that the frequency and output level of the carrier have not been touched). The sound has "thickened" a bit, and maybe you can hear some additional tones. Finally, turn the modulator way up. Run FM4 to listen to the fully modulated sound. Now we hear a sound that might be harder to describe in words, but it has gained more character. What has happened is that the sound has exploded into many other sounds, all splashed across the audible spectrum.

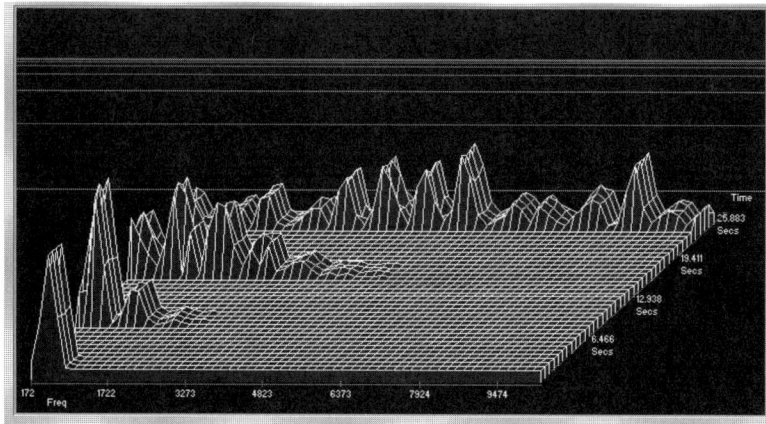

Figure 6-4 Frequency plot of sample tone modulation:
none, light, medium, heavy

You can see the progression between the four sounds we just listened to by comparing their frequency plots in Figure 6-4. Starting at the front, the first simple tone (FM1) appears as a single peak. Moving back into the page, the next grouping shows an additional frequency peak, corresponding to the second audible tone in the lightly modulated FM2 example; a third peak is beginning to develop as well. Moving back to the next grouping, you can see the FM3 example with medium modulation gaining still more frequency peaks. Finally, the mountain range in the back shows the fully modulated FM4 example, with frequency components spread out across the whole spectrum.

This explosion of frequencies is the key to FM synthesis: taking very simple components and straightforward processing techniques and letting them generate complex sounds. These sounds can often mimic real sounds, or they can be something bizarre that no one has ever heard before.

Sounds good so far, right? The problem is that FM is not very intuitive—without an understanding of the mathematics involved, plus a strong background in sound analysis, harnessing the power of FM to do your bidding can be quite a challenge. But don't get discouraged; keep in mind that some of the real fun of FM synthesis is not always knowing what to expect.

ENVELOPES

Before we try changing and creating FM sounds, you need a little more information about sound synthesis. You probably noticed that the last four sound examples would start, run for a few seconds, and then stop abruptly—hardly philharmonic material. Most natural sounds, in contrast, can be broken up into distinct phases where the sound builds in intensity, falls off somewhat, and then settles out completely, all over a period of several seconds. Recall the earlier examples of the flute and cello in Chapter 1. The flute rose very quickly in volume and stayed there until the player stopped blowing. The cello rose more slowly, as the bow started biting into the string, and also fell off slowly as the player continued the stroke. Had the sound gone on, it would have continued to fall off as the player pulled off the bow and the vibration died out. This change in volume over time is the sound's amplitude envelope, or simply, *envelope*.

If you look at the top half of the cello's waveform in Figure 6-5a, you can trace an outline over the peaks of the waves, defining the sound's envelope. Not only does the overall volume of the sound change, but so does the volume of the individual component sounds. If you imagine slicing into the spectrum plot in Figure 6-5b at various frequencies, the cross sections would show profiles that also change over time—but not the same way at all frequencies. So both the overall sound intensity and the mix of frequencies are changing.

To incorporate these time-based changes in FM synthesis, we introduce a missing piece of the puzzle, the envelope generator. Each operator has its own envelope generator to control its output level over time. Figure 6-6 modifies the original synthesizer (Figure 6-3) to include the envelope generator as part of each operator. In FM synthesis, the amplitude envelope, or overall sound

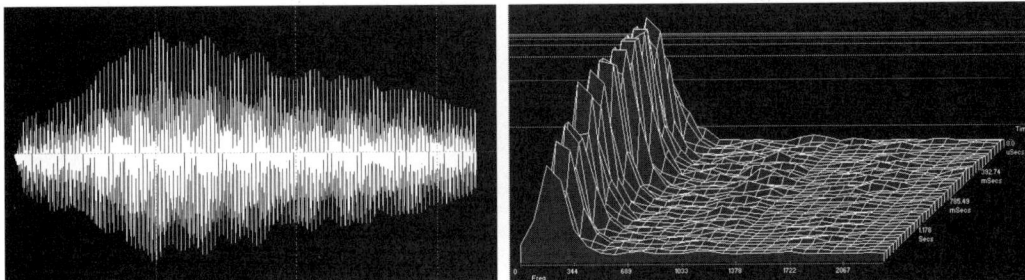

(a) waveform (b) spectrum

Figure 6-5 A cello's plot showing volume changes over time

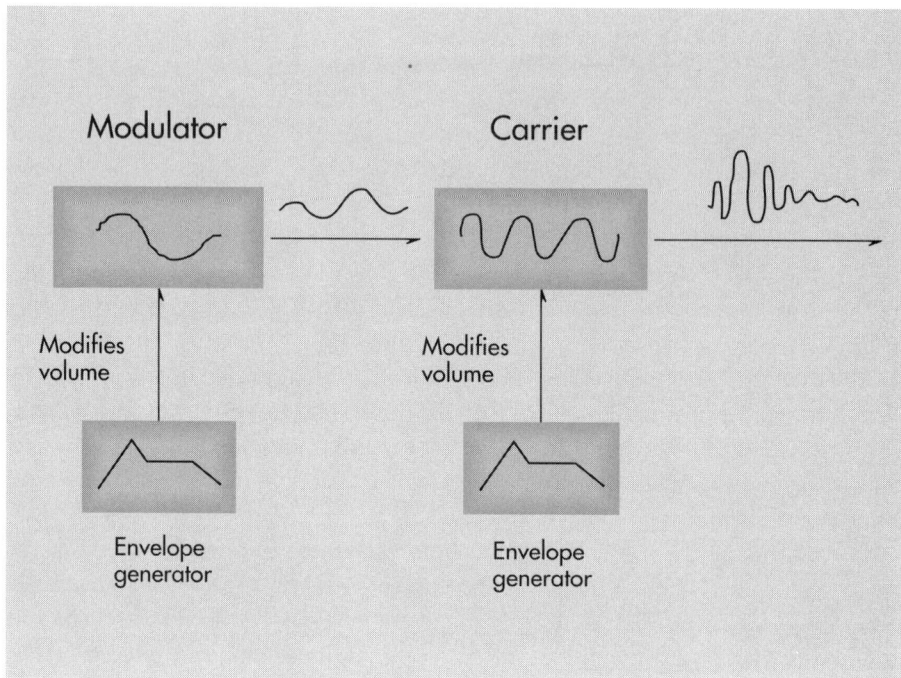

Figure 6-6 FM synthesizer with envelope generators added

level, is mostly influenced by the carrier, while the frequency makeup over time is determined by the modulator. More on this important idea is coming up, but for now, run FM5 to listen to the effect of adding envelopes in the last FM example. It's quite a bit different, isn't it? You'll see in the next section that even slight changes in the envelopes can drastically alter the character of the sound.

CREATING FM SOUNDS

If you've stayed with us so far, you should have a pretty good feel for what sound synthesis is all about and how it differs from the use of digitized audio. Now let's dive into FM synthesis and see if we can master some of its power. Not only can FM produce fairly convincing renditions of real sounds, but it excels at the bizarre. You wanted sound effects—you got 'em!

SBTimbre

The main tool we'll be using to work with FM synthesis is Jamie O'Connell's shareware FM sound editor, SBTimbre. Many example sounds are also included, which can be used as they are or serve as a starting point in making your own sounds. To begin, run SBTimbre by changing to the \SEP\FM directory and typing SBTIMBRE.

SBTimbre is a windowed text application with pull-down menus, and can be used with a keyboard or mouse. There are shortcut keys for some menu functions, with the ones you are most likely to use displayed at the bottom of the screen. For simplicity, we'll assume you are using a mouse for most operations. To move a window, click on its upper border and drag it to a new location. To close a window, click on the small box in the upper-left corner. The two main types of windows we'll be working with are the bank list and timbre editing windows, though we'll also cover some auxiliary functions. The initial screen is shown in Figure 6-7. The configuration window pops up automatically the first time you run the program. For now, just make sure the FM I/O port is set correctly for your sound card (almost always 388) and save the settings; we won't be needing the others.

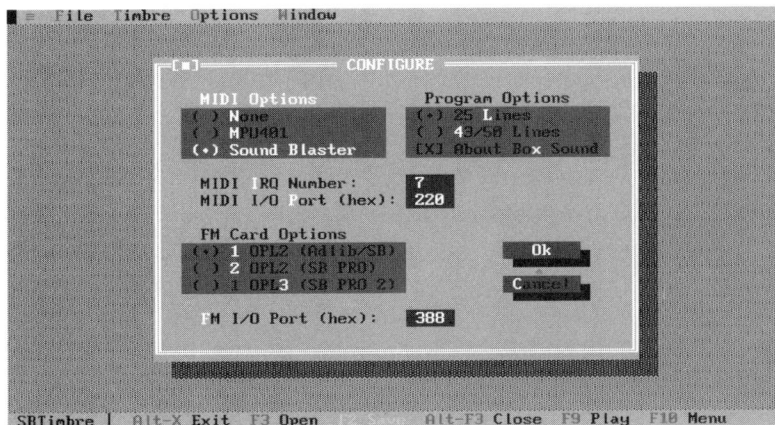

Figure 6-7 SBTimbre's initial screen showing configuration options

The Shotgun Approach

Before looking at FM sounds in more depth, let's go right to the quick-and-dirty (and often the best) approach to creating sounds—random chance. This doesn't sound very scientific, but you'll be surprised at some of the gems it can produce. Use the File menu and select the New option. This displays an empty bank list with a title of NONAME.IBK, as shown in Figure 6-8. A bank contains information on up to 128 sounds, of which 24 are shown at a time. To see more of the bank, use your mouse and the scroll bar on the right, or press (PGDN). Initially the bank appears empty, with numbers identifying the sound slots. You can name sounds for easier reference once you have created them. The bank is not really empty, since each slot initially contains a basic piano-like tone. Click on one of the auditioning buttons on the right to hear a select-

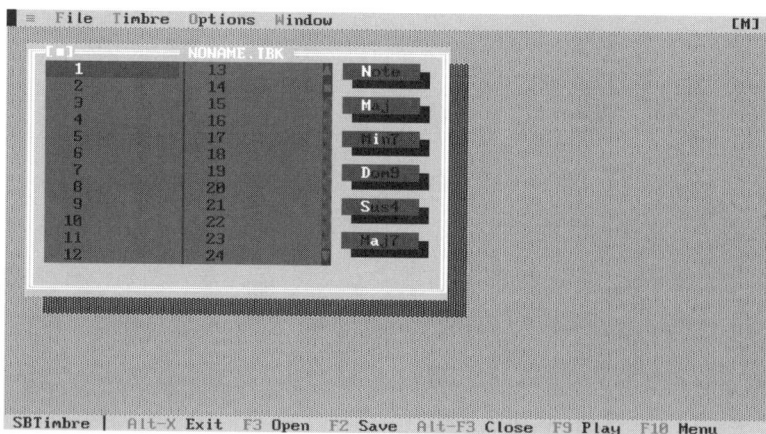

Figure 6-8 New SBTimbre bank list window

76

ed sound. The Note button plays a single tone, and the other buttons play various types of chords. Try these to hear how the initial tone sounds.

Now to mix it up a little. On the Timbre menu, select Randomize and then click OK when asked to confirm the operation. Listen to the first tone again. Then start moving around using your mouse or the arrow keys and listen to some of the other sounds. They all have quite different characteristics, but for the most part, they are variations of the original piano tone. This is very handy when you have a sound that is close to, but not quite what you are looking for. Instead of experimenting with the individual sound controls, you can fill a bank with copies of the closest sound you have using the Timbre menu's Fill bank option (to copy the selected tone to all the other slots), and then randomize the bank. Chances are you will find something suitable just by taking a couple of minutes to scan through the bank, saving hours of trial and error.

Suppose you want some truly different sounds. Randomizing a piano still gets you something that sounds a lot like a piano, but that's only because of SBTimbre's default settings. Go to the Options menu and select Setup Randomize. This new window lets you determine how much of a spread to apply when picking new random control values. Initially, they are all set to a fairly narrow range to produce a close family of sounds. Without actually worrying about what all the strange numbers mean yet, simply make them bigger by typing in new values (or click the up arrow that appears after you select a particular number). For now, don't make the Attack values too large, and do be sure to increase the Modulator Level. Click on OK after you have changed some of the numbers. Now go to the Timbre menu, select Randomize Bank again, and try out the new sounds. Not very pianolike anymore, are they? If all went well, you should have a very bizarre collection of tones, ranging from familiar sounding to not of this Earth.

The Enlightened Approach

Randomizing is an effective way to create new FM sounds, but to take control of the process, it is helpful to understand what is going on "under the hood." Using the File/Open menu option, load the sound bank DEMO.IBK. On the new bank, double-click on the first sound (DEMO 1) or press (ENTER). The Edit Timbre window appears, as shown in Figure 6-9. On this window, you can change all the basic FM sound controls. You may recognize these

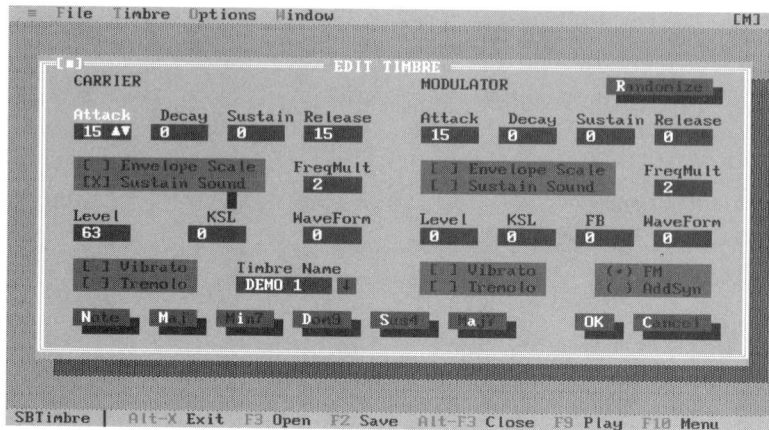

Figure 6-9 SBTimbre's Edit Timbre window showing initial settings

controls from the randomize configuration window; now we'll start to see what the numbers mean.

Timbre collectively refers to those qualities of a sound that distinguish it from some other sound, regardless of pitch or loudness. The Edit Timbre window contains over two dozen items that contribute to a single FM tone. The display is roughly divided into two parts corresponding to the two FM operators: Carrier and Modulator. Recall that the carrier is the basic sound generator, and the modulator rapidly varies the carrier's basic frequency.

Demo 1: Amplitude Envelope

Our first FM setup is a very simple one. In fact, it doesn't use FM at all. You can see this by the fact that the modulator output level is 0. This means that we'll only hear the pure carrier. Click on Note and hold it for a couple of seconds to listen to the sound. You can also press (N), but a mouse works better here because you can hold the note longer. We hear a simple tone that starts immediately and then stops abruptly.

Now let's see what this envelope business is all about. The top four carrier controls—Attack, Decay, Sustain, and Release—determine the sound's overall amplitude envelope. Figure 6-10 represents these control settings graphically as four distinct phases in a typical sound's development over time; let's listen and see how they affect the sound. Play the tone a number of times as you

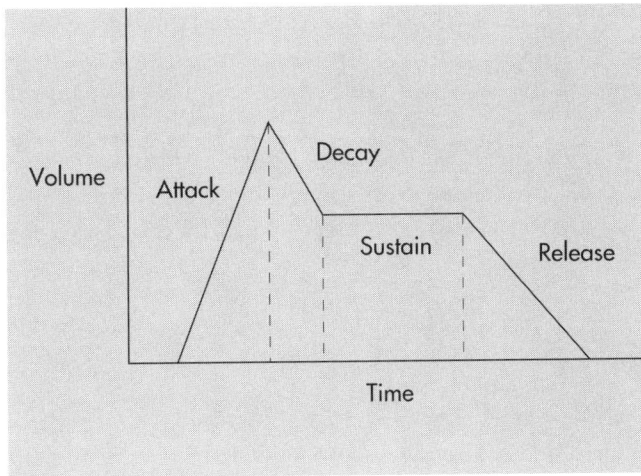

Figure 6-10 Typical sound envelope showing
four loudness stages: Attack, Decay, Sustain,
and Release

reduce the Attack value. Attack determines how long the sound takes to reach
its peak level. A value of 15 is the maximum attack speed. As the attack speed
is lowered, the note takes longer to reach maximum loudness. At very low
attack speeds, it may take quite some time for the note to swell. Attack is very
important in determining the quality of a note; string instruments, for example, have a longer attack, while pianos have a very quick attack.

Return the Attack setting to 15 and move on to Decay. The Decay value
determines how long the sound takes to die out after the initial attack. A
decay value of 0 causes the sound to remain at maximum until you release the
note. Increasing decay values increases the speed of the drop-off. Notice that
as you make Decay larger, the sound shortens, becoming progressively more
percussive, and eventually vanishes.

Sustain is meaningful only if the Sustain Sound option is checked. Sustain
sets the level to which the sound falls after the decay period. If the sustain
level is 0, the sound decays to silence. For higher sustain values, the sound
decays and then reaches a steady level and stays there as long as the sound is
turned on. You may not be able to hear this effect if you are not using a
mouse to hold the Note button down.

Release is the speed at which the sound ultimately drops off after the note
is switched off. A value of 15 turns off the sound immediately, and lower val-

ues let it die out gradually. Release works something like a second decay period. Set Decay and Sustain to 8 and then try smaller values of Release. A longer release could simulate the extended vibration of a plucked or bowed string, for example.

Putting them all together, the basic envelope stages—Attack, Decay, Sustain, and Release (ADSR)—will shape most sounds you'll ever want to create. Some real sounds may have more stages, but these four serve as a good approximation.

DEMO 2: Adding FM

Close the Edit Timbre window and click on DEMO 2 to look at its control settings. The amplitude envelope is already set to values that give us a pleasant, prolonged tone. Listen to it and remember how it sounds. Now go to the Modulator section and begin to increase the output level. It has a fairly wide range, from 0 to 63, with 63 having maximum effect on the carrier. Lower values change the quality of the sound rather subtly, but moving through the higher settings, we hear dramatic changes in the tone. What we hear is the base frequency thickening and spreading out across the sound spectrum. The newly created frequencies are called side frequencies, which spread out above and below the initial frequency. We saw these side frequencies developing in Figure 6-4. A more simplified representation is shown in Figure 6-11.

The quality of the sound is also determined by the relationship between the frequency multipliers (FreqMult) for both the carrier and modulator. Set the Modulator output level to a medium value of 40. Listen to the tone again. Then change the modulator's frequency multiplier from 2 to 3; we get a distinctly bell-like tone. By increasing the modulator level and changing the frequency ratio between the carrier and modulator, we are able to create inharmonic overtones that are characteristic of clanging metal. The term "inharmonic" simply means that the new frequencies are no longer all related to the base frequency by whole numbers. This is just one of the ways in which realistic sounds can be easily generated by FM. Try different settings of the modulator level and frequency multipliers to see how they change the sound.

DEMO 3: Modulator Envelope

Some of the most interesting effects can be achieved using the modulator's Attack, Decay, Sustain, and Release settings. Compared to the carrier ADSR

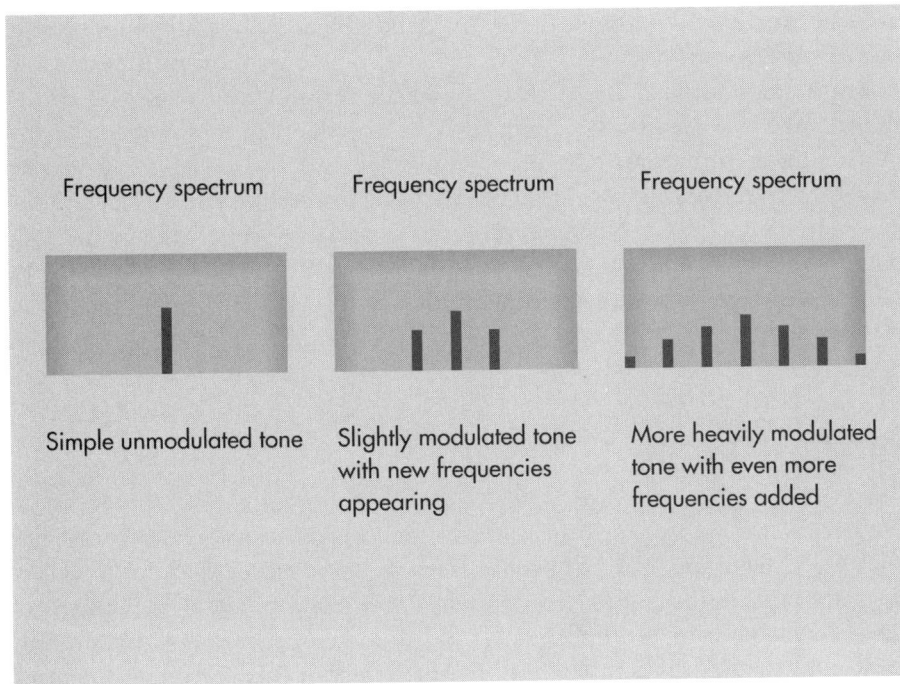

Figure 6-11 Increasing the modulation level in FM synthesis causes additional side frequencies to be generated

settings, where there was a clear relationship to the resulting sound, the modulator's envelope generator's effects can seem bizarre. When looking at real sounds, we have seen that the individual frequency components vary greatly over time. The carrier by itself is rather uninteresting; even adding in the modulation effect, sounds still remain fairly uniform over time. This is where the modulator's envelope comes in.

Close the Edit Timbre display and edit DEMO 3. Try the sound. It's much the same as DEMO 2, but a little lower and a bit twangy. Right now, the modulator envelope is having no unexpected effect because the attack is at maximum and the decay at minimum. That means we have the full effect of the modulator for the duration of the sound. Let's increase the modulator decay time so that its effect drops off (the modulator output goes to 0). Set the decay to 5 and try the sound. Then try it at 6 and 7. Notice how the modulation effect lasts for a shorter time, and then the sound fades into a tone that is more pure. As we increase to 8, 9, or 10, the initial effect gets

even shorter, sounding more percussive, and giving an overall sound that is more drumlike. At maximum decay, we lose the modulation entirely.

Set the modulator decay back to 2 and the sustain and release to 8. Now the sound has a bit of a warbling, or vibrato effect. Let's enhance that by increasing the modulator frequency multiplier to 2 in order to add some more raw frequency material. Then for a more interesting effect, decrease the modulator attack to 3. Now we're sweeping into a quick warbling, and fading out as the warbling slows. Finally, increase the modulator release to 8. Notice how it makes the remaining modulation rush away the moment you release the note.

DEMO 4: Feedback

We have so far ignored one of the most significant controls—modulator feedback (FB). Two-operator FM synthesizers are less flexible than four- or six-operator units in the complexity of sounds they can generate. One way to get more mileage out of two operators is to use some of the modulator's output on itself. The math is complex, but the net effect of this is the equivalent of many parallel modulators acting on the carrier (see Figure 6-12), with a veritable explosion of new frequencies. At the extreme, there can be so many new frequencies that what you hear is just noise. Although you may not realize it, noise itself is useful in producing many real sounds, such as waves crashing, gun shots, the breathy sound that accompanies flute tones, or a snare drum hit.

Edit DEMO 4 and listen to the sound. This curious little rubber band-sounding tone can undergo quite a metamorphosis by increasing the modulator FB value to maximum (7). Try it and see what happens. The kind of percussive, hissing sound that high feedback produces can be used as the basis for a variety of sounds just by making simple changes in the other controls. For example, decreasing the carrier's attack and decay to small values around 2 or 3 makes it sound more like waves swelling and crashing. Then, setting the modulator's frequency multiplier to about 13 produces a sound more like a flying saucer swooshing by. With a little more fussing, we could get helicopters or heavy machinery. Feel free to experiment with some of the other controls. When working with noise, think of it as sculpting: All the sounds are probably already in there; you just need to find them.

In this simple FM operator pair, the modulator output is fed back to itself to modify its own frequency.

The equivalent effect would be achieved using many separate modulators.

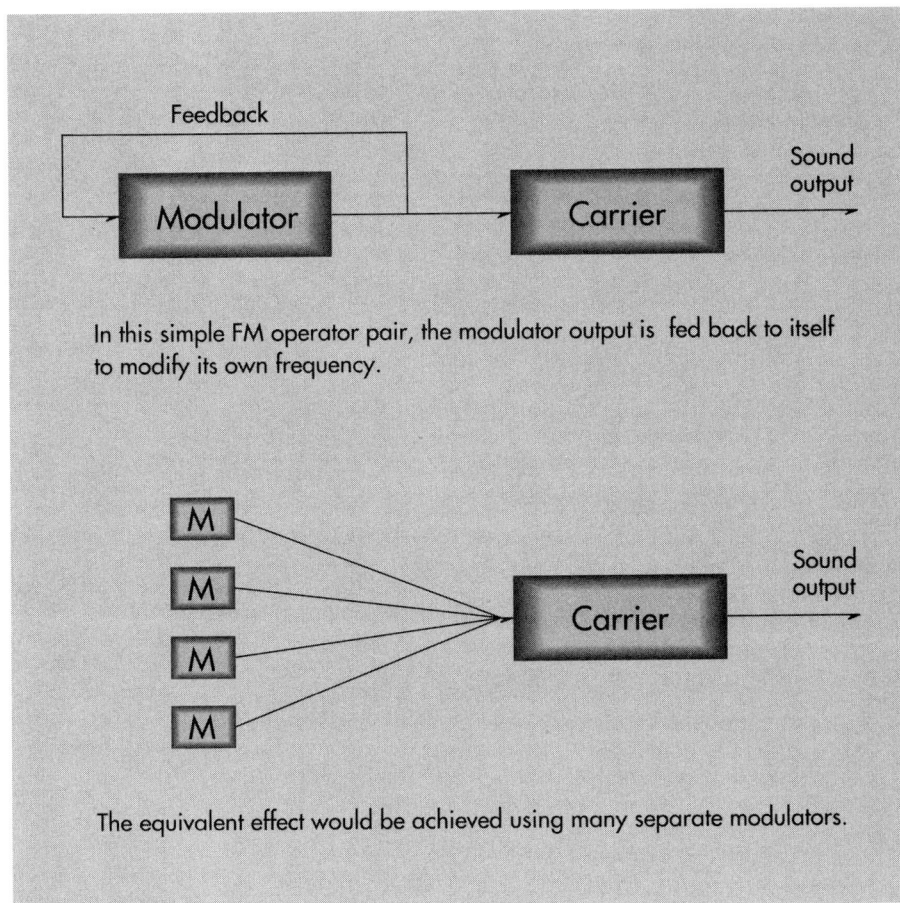

Figure 6-12 Applying feedback to a single modulator to simulate multiple modulators

More control

There are some additional FM controls which will help you refine your sounds. You can use the WaveForm selection to change the basic wave shape of either oscillator. Zero is a simple sine wave, while others are more complex; the main purpose is to give more raw frequency material to work with when creating sounds. The selection of waveforms available depends on the chips your sound card is using. The FM/AddSyn option alters the basic sound

creation method. AddSyn selects Additive Synthesis, an alternate configuration in which the two operators work independently as sound generators. Simply switching modes can have a dramatic effect on the sound.

The remaining controls have less of an impact on the sound. Envelope Scale sounds mysterious, and its effects are not always easy to see. Basically, it shortens the envelope as pitch increases in order to more closely approximate real instruments: It is also used to remove sometimes unwanted side effects of the FM process at higher frequencies. KSL, or key scaling level reduces the output level at higher pitches. Vibrato directly adds a small amount of rhythmic pitch variation. Tremolo varies the loudness in a pulsating manner and is actually a subtle type of envelope effect. All of these options are intended for fine tuning of a sound once the basic settings have been designed; although in some cases they can also have more significant effects (some more FM surprises!).

SBTimbre has a number of features you will find useful when working with FM sounds. It is possible to have multiple sound banks open at one time, so you can mix and match, moving sounds from one bank to another. A handy copy and paste feature on the Timbre menu lets you easily move individual sounds. There is also a Clipboard feature that keeps track of copied sounds. It records a copy of a sound as it existed before you modified it, so that you don't have to worry about clobbering something important. In fact, nothing is really permanent until you save a bank file, so experimentation is encouraged.

We used single note auditioning to listen to selected sounds, but SBTimbre has another feature that lets you listen to musical tones in the context of a song. Selecting the Play option (press (F9)) on the Timbre menu starts up a fractal-based music generator that plays "computed" music—not necessarily Grammy material, but a useful and innovative way to audition sounds. If you have a MIDI keyboard attached to a Sound Blaster or Roland-compatible interface, you can also audition sounds by playing notes directly. MIDI and other settings can be found on the Options menu. See the documentation file accompanying the program for further details.

CONCLUSION

You have seen that FM can be a powerful tool for generating sounds. Not only can it produce many natural sounds, but also some unnatural ones. A large assortment of FM sound in two sound banks is included on the disk for you to use directly or to modify. There are many sound effects and other odd-

ities in SFX.IBK plus numerous musical instruments in INSTR.IBK. These bank files can be loaded directly into SBTimbre and used just like the demo material. In later chapters we'll discuss some applications for FM sounds.

Using FM effectively means experimenting. There's no getting around it. Don't be afraid to try things out. At this point, you may feel a bit like Dr. McCoy puzzling over a Klingon battle console, but don't worry, the worst that can happen is that you'll annoy your neighbors, or send the dog scurrying for cover.

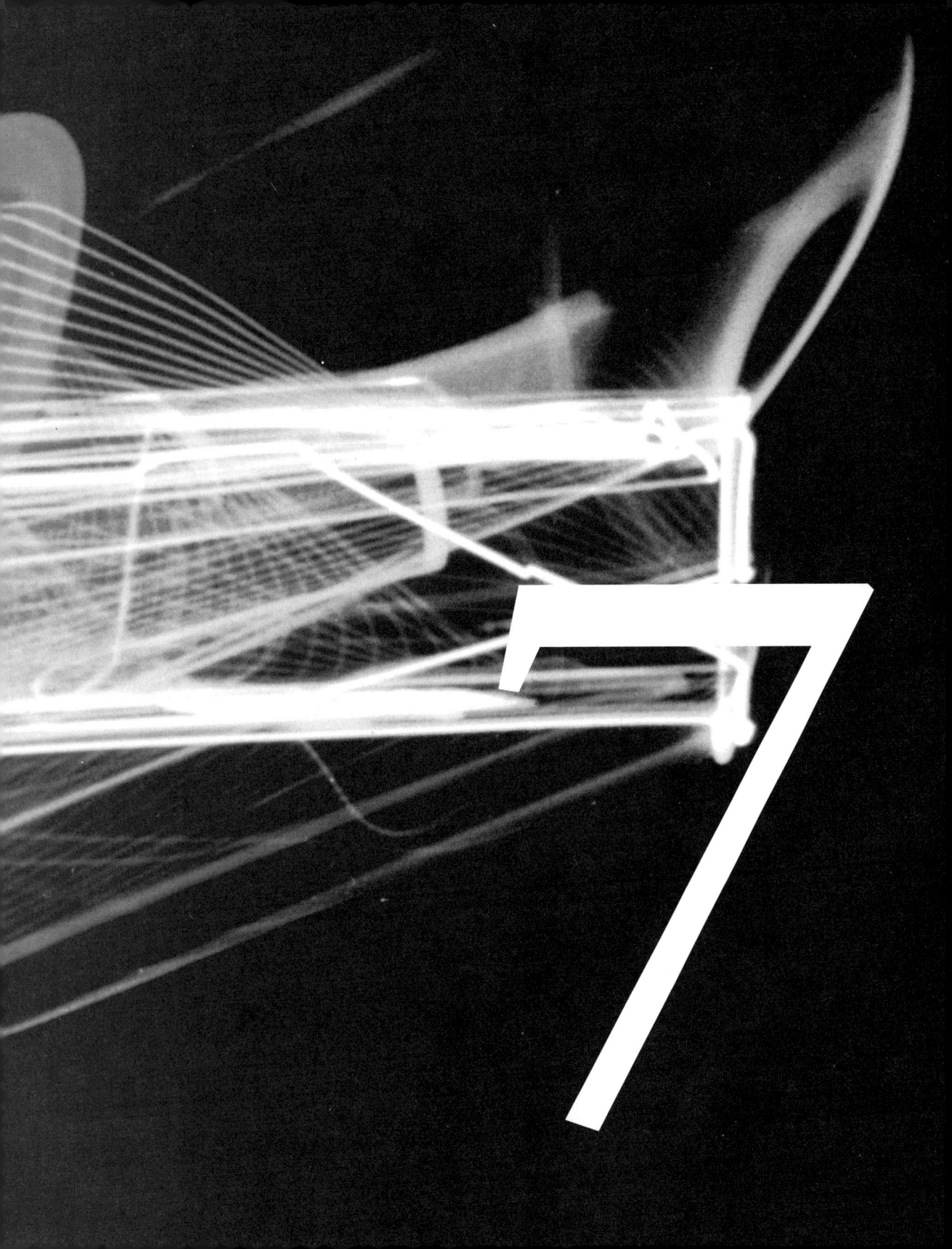

Music

Whether or not you are a musician, you were probably amazed the first time you heard real music being played by a computer. There is something intriguing about machines doing what we have always thought of as distinctly human activities. It may not even be good-sounding music, but still, the novelty has kept many of us glued to our computers for hours just listening in wonder. This chapter looks at how this unlikely marriage between music and high technology came about, and what it means for the typical computer user. For those of you who can never get enough, we'll introduce a couple of handy song file players, one of which will play music for you in the background while you go about your other computing chores.

COMPUTER-CONTROLLED MUSIC

Put aside for the moment what we talked about in earlier chapters on digital audio; when talking about music, we're less interested in how the sounds are made than when they are made. Think about it. Music is much more than simply getting the pitch right—it is first and foremost a matter of timing. The influence of timing is so strong that you can probably recognize a number of popular songs just by listening to someone tap on a table. And as the parent of any bud-

ding musician will testify, getting the notes right, but the rhythm wrong, can make the most well-known song sound like a kitten playing on a piano.

So what can the computer do for us? Simply, it can make sure the right notes get played when they're supposed to be played. Not only can it do that for a simple melody, but being faster than the average musician, it can direct the playing of possibly dozens of different musical parts all at once—bass, drums, lead, fill, or even a whole symphony orchestra. Notice the key point here: The computer is directing the music, not just playing back a digital recording. This is where critical lines between computer sound applications begin to be drawn, and where we start seeing a greater need for sound synthesis.

Digitized audio is fine for many short duration uses, such as voice instructions, sound effects, and brief clips of music; but for long, sustained musical passages, we need to reckon with the limitations and drawbacks of digital recordings. These include

- Potential for noise and distortion

- Very high storage requirements

- Restrictions of digital editing

- High processing overhead

- Smaller selection of tools

- High cost for high quality and function

Fortunately, most of these problems can be avoided. Using synthesizer technology, we can generate musical tones on demand, typically at a much lower cost and with less overhead. At the same time, we get an unlimited ability to change the music. These advantages make synthesized sound a clear choice for many musical applications.

MIDI

We probably have disco to thank, at least in part, for today's music technology. While the idea of disco might make some of you grimace, two new types of electronic music equipment from that era are at the heart of developments that gave us the musical abilities you find in your sound card. They are synthesizer keyboards and automatic accompaniment machines. If you paid much attention to live performances in the late 1970s and early 1980s, you probably noticed musicians showing up with impressive stacks of keyboards. You may have wondered what on earth that guy was going to do with all of them! Play some with his feet? He did command an astonishing array of sound—and that one person could easily substitute for a larger group in a lounge act, with all those different types of sounds plus automated backup and rhythm boxes.

The problem was that every synthesizer manufacturer was topping the other with sounds that were cooler than last month's. Any self-respecting keyboard player had to have those new sounds. Each keyboard had its own special character, and a fairly limited range of available sounds, so all our (now poor) musician could do was keep adding more keyboards—and get dizzy switching between them (see Figure 7-1). Wouldn't it be great if one keyboard could be used to control all the others? Better still, why would they need to be keyboards at all—how about putting just the sound modules in little boxes that don't take up much space? Those very thoughts occurred to the synthe-

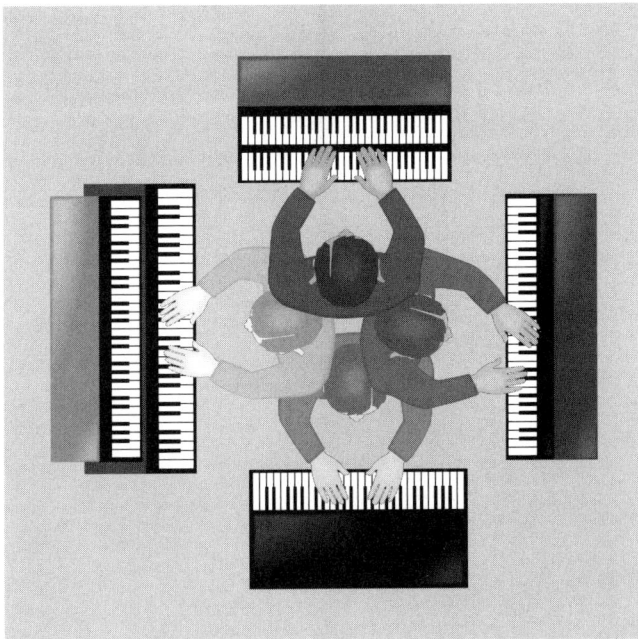

Figure 7-1 In the early years, keyboard players needed lots of instruments to get all the cool sounds

sizer makers, who all rushed off to design ways of plugging instruments together so they could control each other remotely.

As you might expect, a lack of standards would make our musician friend very unhappy when two manufacturers' devices couldn't talk to each other. So it happened that around 1982, a group of the industry leaders got together and worked up a common specification for connecting electronic instruments. This was called MIDI, the Musical Instrument Digital Interface. In its relatively short career, MIDI has become a key ingredient in nearly all professional music recording activities that involve control of electronic music devices. The biggest boon came when people started catching onto the idea that a computer would make an interesting MIDI-capable device itself. The floodgates were open—not only could a single musician control multiple devices, but the computer could participate as a very capable musician's assistant.

MIDI is a fairly simple wiring and data specification, very similar to the serial connections that you might be using to connect to a printer or external modem. The main difference is that it's designed to be strung around from one instrument to the next in a daisy chain. MIDI data consists of short groups of bytes, each representing a command to a MIDI device. The most common of these commands are note-on and note-off sequences. A note-on message tells an instrument to play a certain note, and how loudly. It doesn't say anything else about how to create the note—that's up to the instrument. It only says that it's time to play a note. A little while later, a note-off command can tell it to stop. One other important piece of information contained in the message is the channel. Just like a TV broadcast, each MIDI instrument is tuned to listen on one or more channels and only respond to those it has been set to (see Figure 7-2). MIDI supports 16 channels, so if one instrument in the chain isn't interested in a message, the next instrument in the chain might be. A person wouldn't be able to send musical information on all those channels at once, but a computer certainly could.

Where does the data come from in the first place? Well, if a computer has a MIDI interface, we can plug in a MIDI keyboard and let the computer record the commands as someone plays a song live. The music can be recorded in a track, as if it were on tape, and saved to disk. Keep in mind that MIDI data is very compact, with only a few bytes representing each note played. If we record both the MIDI data and the time at which it was received, it's a simple matter to play it back with the same timing. For multiple parts, the musician can play another track while listening to the first. If that track is set to another channel, it will play back on a different instrument. This can be repeated until the equivalent of a whole ensemble is recorded. Since we've recorded

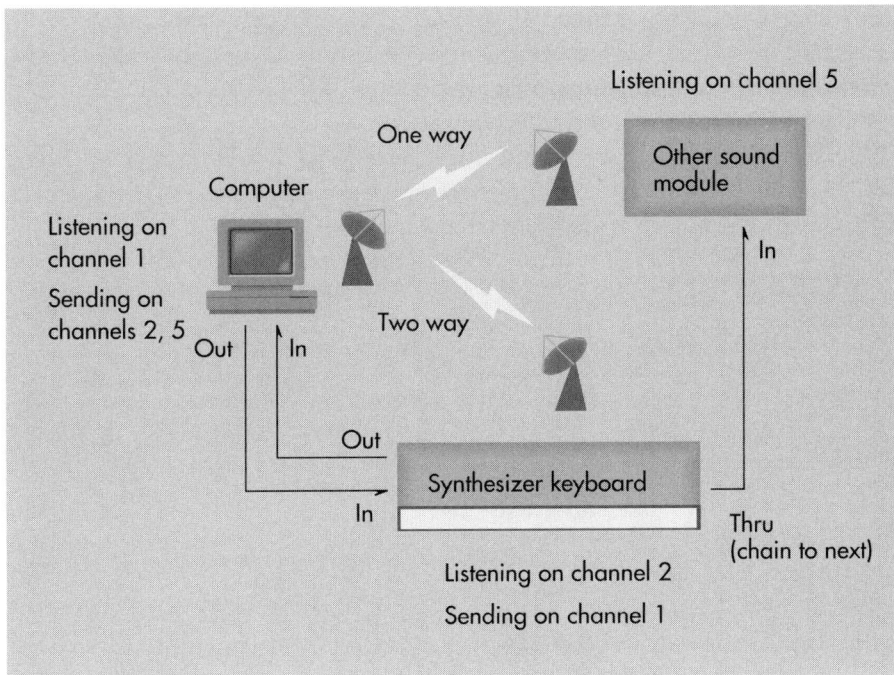

Figure 7-2 MIDI devices chatting, much like TV stations and receivers

simple note event data, it's also easy to go back and edit the data—to correct mistakes, or even to enter a track one note at a time from the computer's keyboard. This is done with special computer programs called sequencers, which are like word processors, but for music. We won't be discussing sequencers in this book, but if you want to create your own music, that's where you'd start. A list of companies selling sequencing software is included in Appendix C.

PLAYING SONG FILES

Just because we've stored MIDI data in a song file doesn't mean that we have to hook up a string of MIDI sound devices to use the data. Many sound cards can simulate a set of MIDI instruments. This is something that is often confusing to beginners. Technically, a MIDI device is something connected at the end of a MIDI cable, so putting sound components inside a computer tends to cloud the issue. MIDI files were designed to be used with MIDI devices, but

they just contain information about musical performances, so we can do what we please with them. That might even be converting the data to conventional sheet music for use by members in a school band. For our purposes here, we'd just like to listen.

Let's get right to it. First, change to the \SEP\MIDI directory. If you haven't already done so at least once, run MIDSETUP to select the type of sound device you are using, with the following command:

```
C:\SEP\MIDI\> midsetup
```

MIDSETUP will ask you a few questions that apply to the programs in this directory:

```
Sound Effects Playhouse MIDI Setup Program
Music interface
        1. AdLib compatible FM (Mono)
        2. Sound Blaster FM (Mono SB 1.0, 1.5, 2.0)
        3. Sound Blaster FM (Stereo SB Pro))
        4. Pro Audio Spectrum FM (Stereo)
        5. Roland MPU-401 compatible MIDI
        6. Sound Blaster MIDI
        7. Pro Audio Spectrum MIDI
        8. IBM PC Music Feature
        9. Key Electronics MIDIator
        10. Generic serial interface MIDI
Enter selection number: _
```

Type the number of the most capable sound interface you have available. If your sound card has stereo capability, be sure to pick a stereo option. Stereo will sound much better, not just because of left/right variations, but because more simultaneous notes are possible.

In some cases, you will see prompts similar to these on the screen:

```
Base Address (220):
IRQ or Com port (7):
```

Enter the base I/O port address and IRQ settings you selected on the interface when you installed it. For the Key MIDIator or Generic serial interface, select the COM port (1 or 2). Don't worry if you're not sure about the IRQ since these programs will work without an IRQ; the base address is what's critical. Press (ENTER) to accept the defaults shown in parentheses.

Play/B and File Formats

Our first MIDI program is a simple command line song player: PLAYB.EXE. All you do to use it is type PLAYB and the name of a song file, and off it goes. It is similar to the TYPE command in DOS, except that it's for auditioning

song files. Play/B stands for Play/Batch, meaning that it's best used in batch files or directly from the command line. It plays a song until completion without any interactive control. You can press ⓠ to quit before the song finishes. Go ahead and try it. Type: PLAYB TELL.

This starts up Rossini's "William Tell Overture" (but you'll probably recognize it as something entirely different). If you look around in the MIDI directory, you'll see quite a number of song files ending with the extension .MID. These are all in the Standard MIDI File format. This is the most common format used for exchanging song files, and it is part of the official MIDI specification. You may, however, come across other song file formats, and this does get to be a bit of a problem. For many years, a file format was not part of the MIDI specification, and all the MIDI software vendors developed their own file formats. In the last few years, most of them have updated their programs to read and write standard MIDI files, so it's not as much of a problem anymore.

One format commonly associated with FM sound cards is CMF, or Creative Music File format. CMF is actually based on the Standard MIDI File format. The difference is that standard MIDI files do not contain any information on how to create the sounds. This would defeat the purpose of a common interchange format, since every device has different ways of creating sounds. CMF files, on the other hand, contain individual FM instrument voice data—the same kind we worked with in Chapter 6. Because it is a common format, the players in this directory will also work properly with .CMF files if you have any (those with an extension of .CMF).

CMF files will sometimes sound better than .MID files on FM cards because the sounds are individually tailored for a particular song. All of the included songs have been set up according to the General MIDI Level 1 Specification. This avoids the need to use CMF format for FM cards. General MIDI is a relatively recent addition to the overall MIDI specification that stipulates which sound numbers correspond to given instruments. A General MIDI song will sound pretty much the same on any General MIDI device. Although FM sound cards are not General MIDI compatible (they may not even be real MIDI devices at all), the included players, like Play/B, will simulate a General MIDI instrument, so they will still sound the way they're supposed to.

Feel free to try Play/B on any of the other songs in this directory. All of the song files beginning with "S_" are short musical clips that you can use to liven up your system; we'll cover this in Chapter 9. All of the other song files are complete pieces. See Appendix B for other sources of MIDI song files, including the latest hits.

95

Play/R: Memory-Resident Player

Play/R is a cousin of Play/B; the "R" stands for "Resident." Play/R is a TSR, or terminate and stay resident, program. What that means is that it loads itself in memory and only shows itself when you want it to. You can go about your business running other programs, and Play/R waits for you to activate it. Its purpose in life is to play song files in the background while you're doing other things.

Running Play/R

Let's go ahead and run PLAYR.EXE and see what happens; simply type PLAYR. Be sure you have already run the MIDSETUP program, as explained earlier in this section. Play/R will indicate that it is loaded and remind you to press (ALT)-(P) to activate it. It then leaves you back at the DOS prompt. At this point, you could run other programs, but for now, we'll just get Play/R's attention from DOS. Hold down the (ALT) key and press (P). When you do that, Play/R pops up a little control panel, shown in Figure 7-3 in the middle of your screen.

Let's start a song playing. Type the name of a MIDI song file (try HOEDOWN) and press (ENTER). The song immediately begins playing. Press (ESC) to dismiss the control panel and return to the DOS prompt. Guess what? The song keeps playing. And it will keep playing no matter what else you do. Type DIR to list the files in the directory. Take note of another .MID file

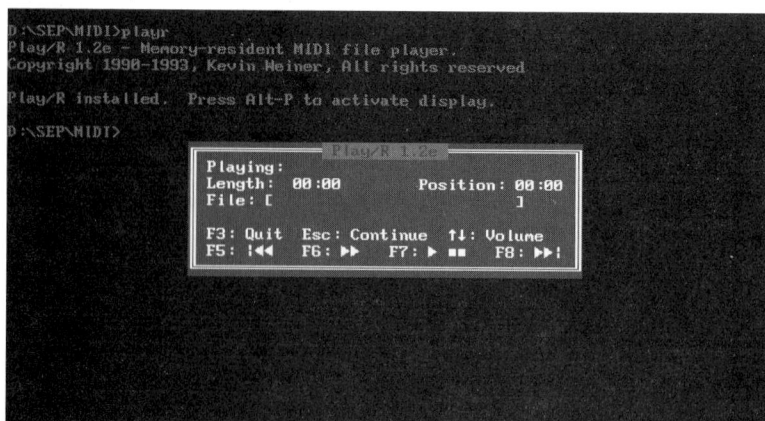

Figure 7-3 Play/R pop-up display for controlling songs playing in the background

96

you'd like to play. Now press (ALT)-(P) again to pop up the Play/R control panel. Type the new file name to start it playing. So far so good?

There's not a lot more to it. If you're tired of Play/R, press (ALT)-(P) and then (F3) at the control panel to exit and remove it from memory. Press (↑) to increase the volume and (↓) to reduce it. The remaining keys are for positioning: (F5) rewinds to the beginning of the song; (F6) skips forward ten seconds; and (F7) toggles between play and pause. The (F5) key has a dual function, and along with (F8), serves as a song skip key when a play list is in use; we'll talk about that next.

Using Play Lists

Play lists can actually be used with Play/R or Play/B; they let you play a series of songs uninterrupted. Play lists are very easy to create: Use any ASCII text editor (or a word processor having an ASCII text export function) and type a list of song file names, one per line up to 30 lines. That's all there is to a play list; just save the list as a text file under any name. To have Play/R load the play list, press (ALT)-(P) and then type the name of the list file in the File area. Be sure to type the character @ in front of the file name to tell Play/R that it is a list, and not an individual song file. For example, the file CLASSIC is a play list file containing names of all the included classical song files. To load it, type @CLASSIC in the File area of the Play/R control panel. Once the list is loaded, play will continue through all the songs without stopping. From the control panel, you can press (F5) at the beginning of a song to go to the previous song in the play list, or press (F8) to go to the next song. The (F6) key will pause play at any time.

If you want to use a play list with the Play/B program, just remember to add the @ character immediately in front of the list file name on the command line. For example, to have Play/B play the songs in TRADITIO (a list of the included traditional song files), type: PLAYB @TRADITIO.

If you forget the @ character in front of a play list file name, the players will assume the file is supposed to be a song. Since they won't find valid song data, they'll give you an error message.

TSR Issues

That's all pretty easy, so what's the catch? Okay, so it's not all roses. TSRs are funny creatures. DOS wasn't really designed to support multitasking

(doing more than one thing at a time). Play/R is a fairly polite DOS citizen, but it does need to get control of the system at regular intervals to make sure play progresses. And it will do that forcibly if necessary. As we said earlier, timing is everything in music playback; if it's not right, your ear will know it. Play/R uses a combination of techniques to make sure timing is uninterrupted. It operates in one of three modes, mode 3 being the default and giving the best timing. But technically speaking, it is also the least safe mode. What that means is that you shouldn't perform any critical operations like backups while Play/R is running. Although there are no known problems during disk I/O, it's still best to play it safe whenever using such a highly active TSR. Where you might see problems is during high-speed modem communications on some systems. Data loss may occur if Play/R has control of the system too long while your computer is receiving data at high speed. It's a good idea to suspend Play/R in such cases. Additional information on Play/R modes and other options is contained in the PLAYR.DOC file in the \SEP\MIDI directory.

The other issue with TSRs is memory usage. Play/R occupies around 64K of memory, which means there is less available for other programs. By default, Play/R uses expanded memory (EMS) for song file storage if it is available. If EMS is not available, even more low memory is required for the song file. If you are running on at least a 386 processor and using a memory manager like QEMM or 386MAX, you may be able to load Play/R in high memory and not use any low memory at all. See the appropriate product documentation for information on how to do this.

CONCLUSION

Even if you're not a musician, some of the fallout from the development of MIDI-based technology can help you enjoy music on your computer. Editing and recording techniques developed over the years have resulted in huge libraries of music files that you can take advantage of using tools like the players in this book. The synthesizer technology developed for professional music applications has found its way into all sorts of inexpensive home equipment, including sound cards. If you are a musician, you'll want to start exploring the incredible power of computer-assisted music production to help in composing, recording, and even sheet music printing. The computer

is the most powerful and flexible musical instrument ever devised, and that's something musicians and non-musicians alike can benefit from.

Software Notice

The Play/B and Play/R programs are neither shareware nor public domain, but have been included, with permission, for free, noncommercial use solely by readers of this book.

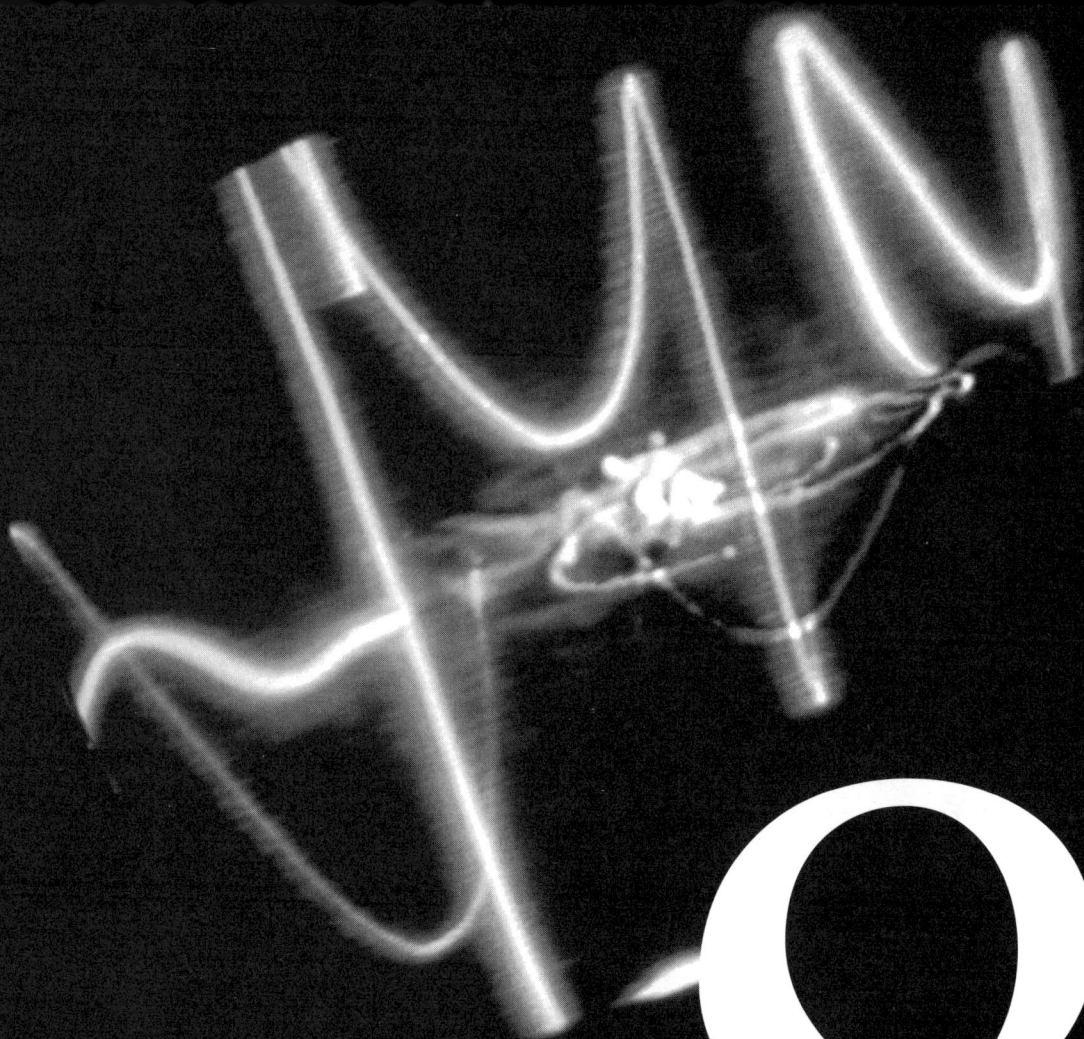

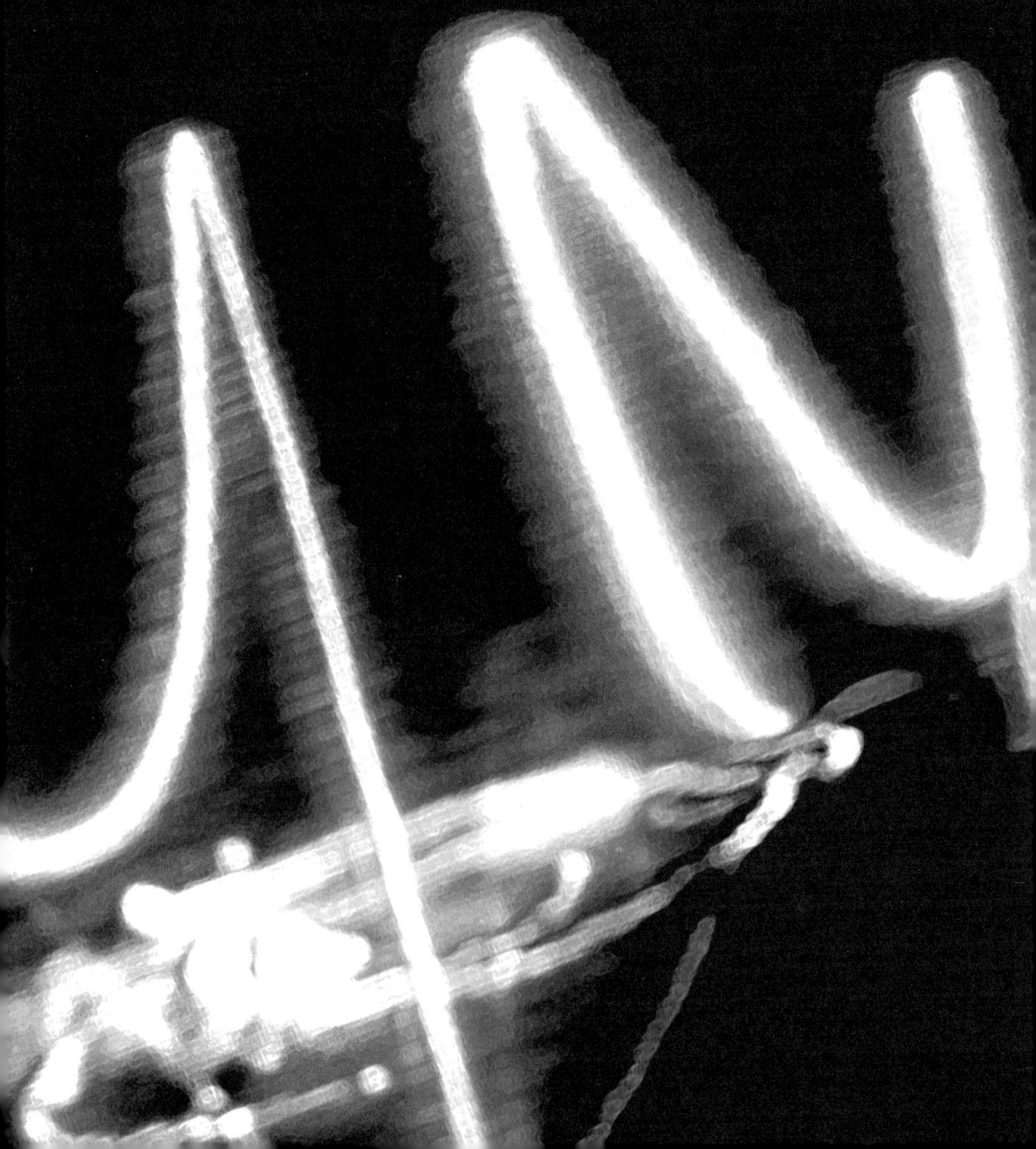

Mod Players

When test pilots speak of "pushing the envelope," they are talking about edging beyond previously tried stress levels—both for the pilot and the aircraft—to expand the known limits of performance. Mod players are a class of programs that truly push the envelope as far as sound hardware and software are concerned. Using very innovative techniques, mod players employ sampled sounds to create real-time musical instrument voices. The sonic results go far beyond what is possible with the built-in FM synthesizer, producing music with a realism that can only be achieved by digitizing a live selection, but at a fraction of the file size. Of course, this magic has its cost: the demands on the CPU are extreme, and the results are often only practical using 386-class machines or higher. We have included two of the best-sounding mod players available for your listening pleasure. If you have a 386 or better, you're invited to see just how far your system can be pushed.

WHAT'S A MOD?

Unlike PC-compatible DOS computers, the Commodore Amiga was designed right from the start with sophisticated sound hardware that allowed it to play four independent channels of digital audio. Each of these channels could be loaded with a digital sound sample and played under control of the processor.

Minimal CPU intervention was required, because after a sound was loaded, the CPU could direct the sound channels to change the pitch, volume, and other effects on their own. One popular music program that supported this hardware was called Soundtracker, and its song files were called modules. The shortened form, "mod," came to be used to describe Soundtracker modules, plus a number of related formats.

What a mod file contains is a set of sampled sounds, typically one for each different instrument used in the song, plus a set of instructions for playing the song. There are many similarities between mod files and the more common MIDI song files. The big difference is that a mod file contains the actual sounds within it, so it will always sound the same no matter where it is played. A mod file also differs somewhat in its song structure, pieces of the song being grouped in short chunks called patterns. The composer can sequence and repeat these patterns to construct a complete song. This makes the amount of note data smaller than it would be in a MIDI file, but mods tend to be larger anyway because of the extra space needed for sound samples.

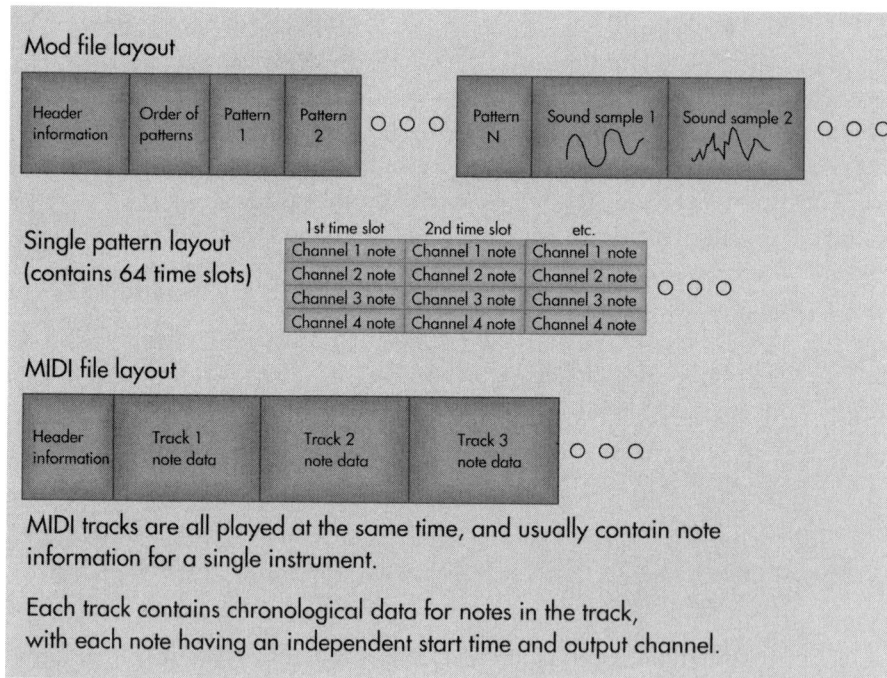

Figure 8-1 Mod file sample- and pattern-based layout compared to simpler MIDI file layout

A single mod file is usually in the 50K to 200K file size range, whereas a MIDI file of 50K is considered big. Figure 8-1 compares the basic layout of mod and MIDI files.

The challenge for DOS machines in playing mod files is the lack of specialized sample playing hardware. Even the typical sound card does not have enough processing capability to simulate the Amiga hardware. But not to be outdone, some clever DOS software designers have taken up the challenge and come up with software solutions that employ the CPU's processing power to make up the difference.

SAMPLE PLAYING

Using real sampled sounds for musical applications is nothing new. MIDI instruments known simply as samplers have been in use for years. These devices are loaded with special signal processors and lots of memory. They can record a digital clip and then change its pitch up or down in real time, usually in response to someone playing on a piano-type keyboard. Using a sampler, it's a simple matter to get a dog to sing "Jingle Bells"—just record the bark, and play it back from the keyboard.

To see how the pitch of a sound sample can be changed, refer to Figure 8-2. Waveform A is the original sample. To double the pitch, or raise it up an octave, just throw away every other sample point and play back the sample at the original sampling rate, as shown by waveform B. You now have twice the number of cycles per second, and so twice the pitch. To lower the pitch an octave, play every point twice at the same sampling rate (waveform C). It's a little more complicated to get pitches in between, but it's still essentially adding or removing points. What we're doing, in effect, is re-sampling the digital waveform to get other pitches.

Musical notes sometimes have a fairly long duration, but we don't want to waste a lot of memory recording, say, ten seconds of a real instrument just to make sure we have enough if the performer decides to hold the note that long. Since most instrumental sounds don't change much after their initial attack and decay stages (usually no longer than a second or two), we can use part of the tail of the waveform and just repeat it. This is called looping, and it lets us get a lot more mileage out of a short sample (see Figure 8-3). Playing the loop at a certain volume level and then fading it can often be a good simulation of the sound's sustain and release stages.

A. Original waveform

B. Every other sample removed = double frequency

C. Every sample doubled = half frequency

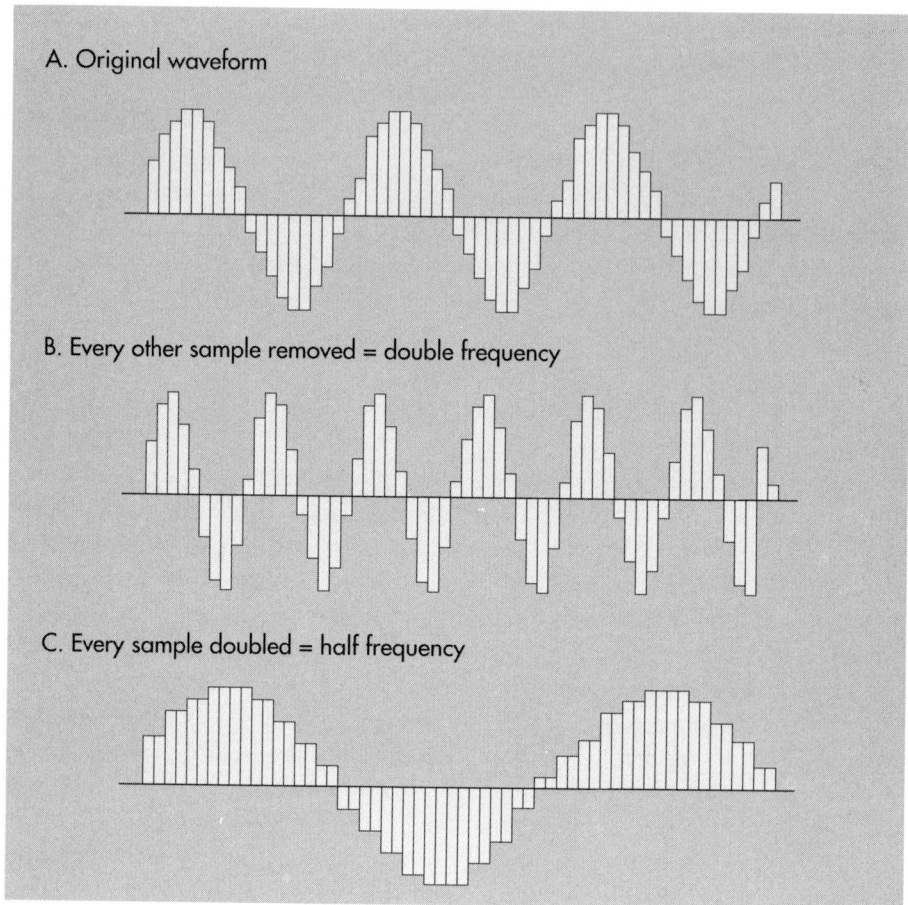

Figure 8-2 Changing the pitch of a sampled sound by removing or adding samples

With a few other processing tricks borrowed from electronic music synthesizers, a sampled sound can be pretty convincing. Samplers have special hardware to do this, and the Amiga has similar capabilities built in. This hardware lets them play multiple sampled sounds simultaneously. On a DOS machine, however, the only way to do all this processing is with software. Mod file players have to pull out all the stops to keep up with the high data rates, and each instruction has to be carefully orchestrated to squeeze out every last microsecond. The sound card's involvement is actually minimal, and really

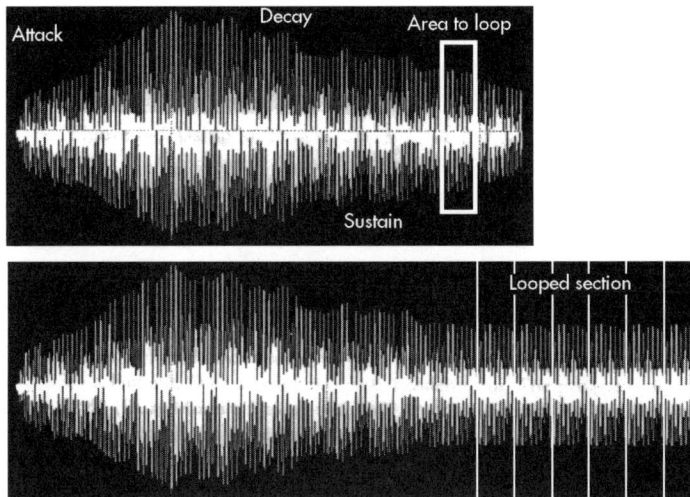

Figure 8-3 Using looping to extend a sound sample

amounts to nothing more than what it would be doing if it were playing a sound file from disk. The difference is that the CPU is busy creating the sound data on the fly!

PLAYING MODS

We've included two related mod players written by a pair of programmers from Finland, Otto Chrons and Jussi Lahdenniemi. The programs are called DMP (Dual Module Player) and PMP (Protected Module Player). They are both based on the same mod playing routines, and differ somewhat in their interfaces and intended uses. The sound quality of both players is excellent due to the highly optimized code, plus direct support of several popular models of sound cards. They do, however, require at least a 386 processor to run, due to the use of 386-specific instructions to improve processing speed.

Jim Young (also known as u4ia) is a talented composer from the U.K. who has graciously allowed us to include several of his original songs in mod format for your enjoyment. As you'll see in one of the pieces, mods aren't limited to strictly musical material—digitized sound samples such as voices are easily included for very impressive effects. Note also how drums and other instruments sound much more realistic than anything that could have been created using FM synthesis.

Dual Module Player (DMP)

Typical mod files contain up to four channels of music, meaning that four separate instruments, or voices, can be playing at once. The name Dual Module Player refers to the fact that DMP can play a special extended mod format consisting of eight channels of music. We'll only be dealing with four-channel music here, but because DMP has been optimized to play at least twice as many channels, it will give great sound quality even on the slowest 386 machines.

The included mod files and players all reside in the \SEP\MOD directory. Change to that directory and run MODSETUP first to make sure the programs can correctly access your sound card. To run DMP, type RUNDMP plus a mod file name. You can also give wildcard file names instead, such as *.mod, to have the program load and play each matching file in succession. For example, type RUNDMP *.MOD and press (ENTER) to play all the included mod files.

RUNDMP is actually a batch file that adds setup options to the real program, DMP.EXE. The DMP.DOC file explains the various options available if you'd like to run the program directly choosing special settings. Figure 8-4 shows the DMP display with a song loaded and playing.

The second line of the display shows information about the song, including its title and size. The line below that gives song progress and other playback information. Pattern shows the current chunk of the song being played, plus

Figure 8-4 Dual Module Player display

the total number of patterns in the song. Row is the current note position within the pattern. Time is the elapsed time since the beginning of the song. Volume indicates the loudness, with 64 being the maximum. Rate is the playback sample rate in samples per second.

The gray section shows information about each channel. On the left is text associated with the current instrument being played. This may be the name of an instrument sample, or any other text the composer decided to include. Following the instrument name are the name of the note in progress, the channel volume, the type of special effect (if any) being applied to the note, and a bar graph of the channel volume.

The bottom section of the screen lists each of the instruments included in the file. Typical mod file formats include up to 16 or 32 instrument samples. Each sample slot may contain the name of the instrument, or again, any other text the composer wanted to insert. As the song calls for specific instruments, DMP highlights those names, as well as showing them in the channel status area above.

Table 8-1 lists the more common keystroke commands you may use while playing. Other commands are listed in DMP.DOC.

Key	Function
H	Show help information
P	Pause (any other key resumes)
N	Load next song
S	Stereo on/off
F	Filter on/off (SB Pro only)
D	Go to DOS (type EXIT to return to player)
←, →	Previous, next pattern
+, -	Increase, decrease volume
ESC	Exit program

Table 8-1 Common DMP commands

Protected Module Player (PMP)

You'll find the operation of PMP to be very similar to DMP. One obvious difference between them is that PMP runs in a graphical display mode, with four larger volume meter bars. These pulsate with the music and give the effect of a color organ (good for parties). You'll need a VGA display to run the program because of this and, like DMP, it also requires a 386 processor. PMP uses the processor in protected mode, hence the name. Protected mode lets you use all the high memory available on your machine for loading mod files. One advantage of this is that the mod files you select can reside in memory for quicker startup. The other advantage is that you can switch to the DOS prompt (by pressing (D)), letting play continue in the background, and still have plenty of memory to run other applications.

To run PMP, type RUNPMP and the name of a mod file (or a wildcard pattern to load multiple files). RUNPMP is a batch file that runs the real program, PMP.EXE, with setup options. See PMP.DOC for information on additional command options.

Figure 8-5 shows the PMP program's display. It includes slightly less information than DMP: the song position at the top, list of songs loaded on the right, instrument list on the bottom, and volume bars in the large middle section. The keystroke commands are nearly identical to those in DMP (see Table 8-1). Two additional keys that are useful are (B) to toggle the volume bars off

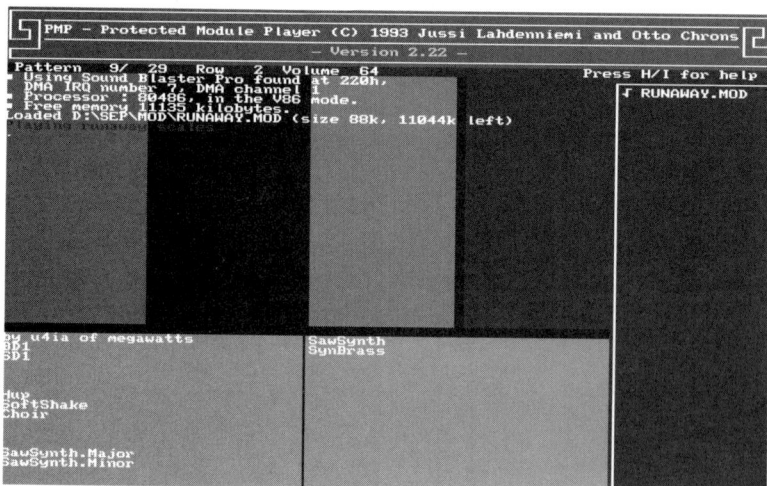

Figure 8-5 Protected Module Player display

and on, and Ⓒ to clear the message area, which happens to be in the same place as the volume bars. The bars are transparent and overlay any messages from the program. You may want to turn off the bars with Ⓑ to make messages easier to read, or use Ⓒ to clear messages and keep the bar display neater.

CONCLUSION

If you've never heard a mod file playing on your sound card, you're bound to be impressed with the quality of this live music. If you're intrigued by the possibilities mod files present, see Appendix B for more sources of music. In general, mod files provide a new degree of realism and flexibility in composing songs for sound cards of modest cost. They are only matched by MIDI files played on more expensive sound cards that have high-end synthesizers or sample-playing hardware built in. Those options typically do not provide the capability of easily mixing in the digitally recorded sound effects that add dramatic impact found in mod songs. Although the quality of mod sample playback is limited compared to dedicated sound options, the improvement over conventional FM sound is remarkable and well worth considering for your musical applications.

9

Adding Sound To DOS

Let's face it, DOS isn't the most exciting environment around. Some day the old C:\> prompt might fascinate a future archaeologist, but right now, DOS is just plain dull. Fortunately, we can take some simple steps to liven it up by breaking the silence and getting it to chime in with some strategically placed sounds. You didn't think we'd let all the cool sounds we've been playing with go to waste, did you?

This chapter will explore a few easy ways to get DOS to make noise. With some basic tools, you can get your favorite programs to speak up and cheerfully announce themselves when they start, or to go away grumbling. We'll do a little work under the hood and show you how to automatically produce sound when certain DOS events occur, such as files being read or deleted, or directories being changed. We'll even see how you can create a makeshift musical instrument out of your computer's keyboard that's available whenever you need it. Yes, DOS can be taught to speak, and you're the master.

BATCH IT

The batch file capability in DOS is an underused tool that can make the environment much easier, more productive, and certainly more pleasant. Batch files are the fastest, easiest, and safest way to add sound to a typical program in DOS. We'll look at a more high-tech solution in the next section, but for now, let's explore the lowly batch file.

Using DOS Batch Files

If you're a casual DOS user, it's possible that you've never created a batch file, or realized when you were using one. The concept is simple: Instead of retyping a series of DOS commands every time you need them, you type them into a file once and save it. You can create batch files in any text editor, such as DOS' EDLIN (if you have the patience), EDIT (in DOS 5 and higher), or in your favorite word processor (if it has the ability to save or export ASCII text files). You type the commands in the file, as you would at the DOS prompt, and then save the file (in text mode if you're using a word processor), giving it an extension of .BAT. The extension tells DOS that the file contains commands and that it can "run" the file.

At this point, your batch file is essentially a new program. When you type its name (the extension isn't necessary when running it), DOS executes the commands in the file as if you had typed them at the prompt yourself. You can run it any number of times, and it will always execute the same series of commands. There are many helpful features that you can use in batch files, but this is most of what you need to know for our purposes here.

And what exactly are those purposes? How do batch files relate to sound at all? Batch files really have nothing special to do with sound, but since you can use them to combine a series of programs, you can take one of your regular applications and surround it with programs that do produce sound. For example, suppose you use a word processor called ABC Deluxe, and to run it you type ABCD. Instead of the normal quiet startup, you want to make a statement about having to be inside working on a sunny day, so you choose a sound file called CUCKOO.VOC (in the \SEP\VOC directory) as your new startup sound. To do this, we'll need to produce a stand-in for ABCD—a batch file called RUNABCD.BAT. It contains two lines and looks like this:

```
\SEP\VOC\PLAYVOC \SEP\VOC\CUCKOO.VOC
ABCD %1 %2 %3
```

116

Now, to run the program, type RUNABCD instead of ABCD. The first line runs a program we haven't seen yet called PlayVOC. It's very simple to use—just give the name of a VOC file on the command line and it plays it. The program is found in the \SEP\VOC directory, so if you're not in that directory, you need to include the directory name as part of the command.

The second line runs the ABCD program when the VOC file stops playing. The percent codes are place holders, in case you ever use any file names or options on the ABCD command line. If you use more than three, add some codes (%4, %5, and so on), or if you use fewer or none at all, take some off. If you sometimes type ABCD and a file, just type RUNABCD and a file now. For example, if you typed ABCD MYDOC before, type RUNABCD MYDOC now. MYDOC is substituted for the %1 on the ABCD line in the batch file. If you happen to use a second file name or option, it replaces the %2, and so on. Any leftover percent codes are ignored.

With a simple modification, you can have a sound played when the ABCD program ends. To do this, add a third line to the batch file that plays a sound file. When you exit the ABCD program, the next line in the batch file executes, so there's no reason it can't be another sound command. That's really all there is to it. Well, almost.

Staying on the Path

We need to talk a bit about the dreaded DOS search path—you'll need it to run your batch files efficiently. The path is simply a string of directory names that DOS uses when it's searching for a program you just told it to run. For example, since you originally typed ABCD to run that word processor, ABCD is probably a program file called ABCD.EXE, and if it's not in your root or current directory, it has to be in some other directory in your path. Otherwise, DOS couldn't find it when you type ABCD.

In order to let our new RUNABCD.BAT file run by typing RUNABCD, no matter what the current directory is, RUNABCD.BAT must be in a directory in the path. If you only plan to use a few batch files, often the root directory (\) is the best place to create them. But if you expect to create a lot of batch files, make a separate directory called \BAT (for example) to help keep your files better organized. The \BAT directory must then be in your path. To put it there, you must edit the AUTOEXEC.BAT file in your root directory. This is just another batch file, but it's special in that it's always the first thing run by DOS when your system starts up. In it, you'll probably find a line starting

with PATH=, or if not, place one at the top of the file yourself. It might look something like this after we're done adding \BAT:

```
PATH=C:\;C:\DOS;C:\BAT;C:\ABCD
```

The individual directories, separated by semicolons, tell DOS to search for programs (including batch files) in root, DOS, BAT, and ABCD—in that order. The first program in one of those directories that matches the name you typed is the one DOS will execute. We could have called our batch file ABCD.BAT in order to keep the customary name, because the batch file is in a directory that comes before the program directory and will be found first. But do you see a problem here? What happens when the ABCD line in the batch file is executed? Right, it gets the batch file again first and runs it again, and again, and again; until you get tired and shut off the machine. The cure is simple: Change the ABCD line in the batch file to include its directory name, thus bypassing the search path:

```
\SEP\VOC\PLAYVOC \SEP\VOC\CUCKOO.VOC
\ABCD\ABCD %1 %2 %3
```

A Batch of Sound Programs

After this quick lesson in DOS, you're armed with enough information to start creating your own batch files to produce sounds when you want them. To help you do this, we've included three simple sound playing programs: PlayVOC, Play/B, and PlayFM. You saw the new program PlayVOC used in the previous section, and may recall Play/B from Chapter 7. We'll review them briefly here, and introduce another new program, PlayFM, for playing simple FM sounds.

PlayVOC

We just used the PlayVOC program in our batch file sample—it simply plays a voice (.VOC) file that you type in on the command line:

```
PLAYVOC file.VOC
```

The PlayVOC program resides in the directory \SEP\VOC, along with a collection of sample voice files with names such as BARK.VOC, CHOPPER.VOC, ENGINE.VOC, and SIREN.VOC. Be sure you've run the VOCSETUP program in that directory once so that PlayVOC will be set up correctly for your sound card. PlayVOC is able to play any of the files included with this book with the .VOC extension. You can also record as many sounds of your own as you'd like using the Blaster Master program (see Chapter 3).

Play/B

We first saw the Play/B program in Chapter 7. If you'd like to add a musical flourish to a batch file, pick a short MIDI file and let Play/B play it for you. Be sure to check out some of the song files in the \SEP\MIDI directory starting with "S_". These are all musical snippets, well suited for use in batch files when you want a brief musical moment. To play a song file, simply type PLAYB and a .MID file name. For example:

```
PLAYB 2001.MID
```

See Chapter 7 for detailed information on using Play/B and MID files.

PlayFM

The PlayFM program is another simple sound file player. In this case, the sounds are single FM instrument voices such as the ones we worked with in Chapter 6. The PlayFM program resides in the \SEP\FM directory, and you'll need to use the SBTimbre program (also in that directory) to produce sound files for it. Recall that we worked with .IBK, or instrument bank files. PlayFM uses single instruments extracted from an .IBK file into smaller SBI (Sound Blaster Instrument) format files. Run SBTimbre and load an instrument bank. Then audition and select sounds you are interested in using with PlayFM. Choose Export SBI from the File pull-down menu to write the currently selected instrument to an .SBI file. Once you have some .SBI files created, exit SBTimbre, and to play one, just type PLAYFM and the .SBI file name.

If you just give a file name, PlayFM plays the instrument for one second, assuming middle C as the pitch (even though it may not be a musical instrument sound). To change the duration of the tone, add the number of milliseconds (1 second equals 1000 milliseconds) following the file name. To change the pitch, include a note number from 24 to 107 after the duration. For example, to play the tone from a file, ACGRAND.SBI, for half a second using note number 62 (the D above middle C), type

```
PLAYFM ACGRAND 500 62
```

Instead of using note numbers, you can specify note names. Note names consist of the note letter, a sharp (#) or flat (b) indicator, and the note's octave number. Middle C starts octave 3. Here are some example note names followed by their numbers:

```
C0      24      (Lowest)
C#0     25
Bb2     58
B2      59
C3      60      (Middle C)
B6      107     (Highest)
```

119

Using a note name, the previous PlayFM command line would be:

```
PLAYFM ACGRAND 500 D3
```

If you use a note name or number to change the pitch, you must include a duration in milliseconds.

Before running the PlayFM program, be sure you've run the FMSETUP program once in the \SEP\FM directory to set it up for your sound card.

Putting it Together

Including any of these sound programs in a batch file that runs a program, you can easily add startup and exit sounds to programs. Don't forget to give full directory names for sound or program files so that you can run the batch files anywhere. Here's a simple variation of our RUNABCD.BAT file that starts the program with a high-pitched FM tone and ends it with a low-pitched one. Note the use of the \SEP\FM and \ABCD directory names.

```
\SEP\FM\PLAYFM \SEP\FM\ACGRAND 2000 C4
\ABCD\ABCD %1 %2 %3
\SEP\FM\PLAYFM \SEP\FM\ACGRAND 2000 C1
```

Just like any other batch file, you can also play sounds from within your AUTOEXEC.BAT file. Placing one of the sound playing commands near the beginning, you can have any type of sound greet you when your system starts up.

To review, here are the command line sound players included:

PlayVOC   For .VOC files (digitized sound)
Play/B   For .MID files (MIDI and CMF song files)
PlayFM   For .SBI files (FM sounds)

In addition, your sound card may have come with similar players that you should try out because they may be better tuned to your specific hardware than the generic players we've included.

PATCH IT

Creating batch files is the simple, brute-force method of associating sounds with DOS programs. Now we'll look at a type of sound player that hooks into your system and becomes part of DOS itself. This program, called FMSYS, loads into memory as a TSR (terminate and stay resident) program. It continuously monitors certain types of DOS events that you select, and when they occur, it plays FM sounds. While it is possible to have such a program play

.VOC or other types of sound files, that is potentially less safe because of the extra background CPU and disk activity. FM offers a wide variety of interesting sounds and requires no system overhead because the sounds are generated on the sound card.

As in the last section, you'll need a set of FM sound files. You can create your own new sounds or select ones from the sample instrument bank (.IBK) files we've included. Use the File/Export SBI menu selection in SBTimbre to write individual .SBI files of the sounds you'd like to use. The FMSYS program resides in the \SEP\FM directory, and if you haven't run the FMSETUP program at least once, you should do that now to set up FMSYS for your sound card.

Event List

FMSYS needs to know what events you want it to monitor and what sounds to use when those events occur. You provide this information through an event list file. This is a simple text file, created using a text editor or word processor that can export text. It contains a list of events and FM sound files to associate with them. A single event line in the file might look like this:

```
RUN FORMAT.COM \SEP\FM\ACGRAND 1000 C3
```

Each event starts with a special key word, in this case RUN. The RUN event requires the name of a program file and then the specification for an FM sound. The sample event says: "When the program FORMAT.COM is run, play the FM sound file \SEP\FM\ACGRAND.SBI for 1000 milliseconds using note C3 (middle C)." Notice that the FM specification part is exactly the same as for the PlayFM program from the last section. You don't have to include the duration and note; if you don't, the program assumes 1000 and C3.

Another type of event is the KEY event. Here is an example that instructs FMSYS to play TOMTOM.SBI when (ALT) and (F10) are pressed together:

```
KEY ALT-F10 \SEP\FM\TOMTOM
```

Note, however, that once you assign a keypress sequence to a sound, that key sequence cannot be used for anything else. Be sure you don't need the particular key sequence in an application you plan on using while the KEY event is in effect. Any of the displayable keys on the keyboard (not including the numeric keypad), plus the (F) keys, are candidates for sound attachment. As the example shows, you can define the key as a combination of (ALT) and a normal key. In fact, you can use any combination of (ALT), (SHIFT), and (CONTROL), along with a normal key to make up a key definition. For example, CTRL-ALT-A

means pressing (CONTROL), (ALT), and (A) at the same time. Although you can use any key, such as (A), by itself, it may not be a good idea. You'll probably need the key at some point, and you will get an irritating sound when you press it. Note that you can only use the base key once; for example, if you use (CONTROL)-(SHIFT)-(B), you can't use (ALT)-(B) for a different sound.

Table 9-1 shows all the possible event types, their key words, what kind of item follows the key word, and whether an FM file name is required. Where you see "pattern" listed, you can give a DOS wildcard specification, such as *.* (meaning any file).

Event Type	Keyword	Item	FM File
Running a program	RUN	File or pattern	Yes
Opening a file for any purpose	OPEN	File or pattern	Yes
Deleting a file	DELETE	File or pattern	Yes
Renaming a file	RENAME	File or pattern	Yes
Ending any program	END	none	Yes
Changing a directory	CD	Directory or pattern	Yes
Removing a directory	RD	Directory or pattern	Yes
Changing drives	DISK	none	Yes
Pressing a key	KEY	Key name	Yes
Unloading FMSYS	UNLOAD	Key name	No

Table 9-1 FMSYS event types

Running FMSYS

To run the program and load it into memory, type FMSYS and the name of an event list file. A sample file called EVENTS has been included in the \SEP\FM directory. To use it, type FMSYS EVENTS and press (ENTER).

122

Here are the event lines contained in the sample file. Everything after a semicolon on a particular line is ignored as a comment.

```
; Sample FMSYS event file
;
RUN \DOS\*.* BELL4 100      ; Short bell when any DOS program runs
RUN *.* ENERGIZE 300        ; Transporter-type sound when any
                            ;  other program runs
OPEN *.WKS SHOT             ; Fire a shot when a spreadsheet is accessed
RENAME *.* WHOOP            ; Whoop when renaming any file
END SCREECH                ; Screech when any program ends
                            ;  (Note: No program name allowed)
CD \ BUZZER                ; Sound buzzer when changing to root dir
CD * JUMP                  ; Bouncing sound when changing directory
RD * CHIME 100             ; Chime when removing a directory
DISK BOING 200             ; Boing sound when changing drives
                            ;  (Note: No file item, just FM name)
KEY ALT-F1 ACGRAND 500 C2  ; Assign piano sound to Alt-F1
KEY ALT-F2 FLUTE 2000 C3   ; Assign flute to Alt-F2
UNLOAD ALT-X               ; Unload FMSYS when Alt-X is pressed
```

These FM sound file names are examples that have already been extracted from the instrument banks; you could pick any .SBI file names you have created or extracted from one of the supplied bank files. Don't forget to give a directory as part of the .SBI file name if you are running FMSYS from a directory other than the one containing the instrument files. The .SBI extension on FM files is not needed; it is assumed.

Note the special UNLOAD key. If you define one, pressing the key sequence you give will terminate the FMSYS program and unload it from memory. In this example, pressing (ALT)-(X) would remove the program. You can also type FMSYS -R to remove the program, but as we'll see shortly, that's not always possible.

When you define multiple file or directory events using the same key word, place events with specific file names first, followed by any patterns. FMSYS matches events in the order they appear in the file. If a file name matches a general pattern first, a more specific file name might be missed. The RUN lines in the sample event list demonstrate this:

```
RUN \DOS\*.* BELL4 100      ; Short bell when any DOS program runs
RUN *.* ENERGIZE 300        ; Transporter-type sound when any
```

If the order of these lines had been reversed, the \DOS directory line would never get processed because *.* matches any program in any directory.

You can start up FMSYS at any time, but if you always want it to be in effect, the best time to run it is at system boot time, as part of your

AUTOEXEC.BAT file. Let's assume you have all the necessary files in \SEP\FM, including an event list called MYLIST. Then just insert the following lines in AUTOEXEC.BAT:

```
CD \SEP\FM
FMSYS MYLIST
CD \
```

By first changing to the \SEP\FM directory, you make sure all the files are accessible at the time FMSYS runs, and avoid having to spell out the directory name for each instrument file in the event list. If you are using a 386 memory manager, feel free to load FMSYS into high memory to avoid taking away low memory from other applications. See your memory manager or operating system manual for information on doing this.

Portable Piano

The following sample event list file, called PIANO, can be found in the \SEP\FM directory. It converts your keyboard into a three-octave piano by reassigning most of the characters in the four main rows. Here is an excerpt from it:

```
key       a       acgrand      400      b1
key       z       acgrand      400      c2
key       s       acgrand      400      c#2
key       x       acgrand      400      d2
key       d       acgrand      400      eb2
key       c       acgrand      400      e2
key       f       acgrand      400      f2
key       v       acgrand      400      f2
key       g       acgrand      400      f#2
key       b       acgrand      400      g2
key       h       acgrand      400      g#2
key       n       acgrand      400      a2
key       j       acgrand      400      bb2
key       m       acgrand      400      b2
key       k       acgrand      400      c3
key       ,       acgrand      400      c3
key       l       acgrand      400      c#3
key       .       acgrand      400      d3
key       \;      acgrand      400      d#3
key       /       acgrand      400      e3
    . . .
key       [       acgrand      400      b4
key       =       acgrand      400      c5
key       ]       acgrand      400      c5
unload f3
```

124

To use PIANO, change to the \SEP\FM directory and type FMSYS PIANO. This event file arranges the keys starting with note C2 at the left of the bottom row, and uses certain keys in the row above it for sharps and flats (the black keys on a piano). It continues up the scale with the row starting at Q (see Figure 9-1). Notice the "\" character in front of the semicolon for the D#3 key. This keeps the semicolon from being treated as the beginning of a comment and eating up the rest of the line. Also notice the UNLOAD F3 definition at the very end of the file. This is very important because once FMSYS starts, you won't be able to type any commands (such as FMSYS -R) to remove the program. Since we defined an unload key, just press (F3) to exit.

You could make some simple changes that would let the piano stay around all the time without interfering with your normal typing. Just by adding CTRL-SHIFT- in front of each regular key in PIANO, you would have to hold (CTRL) and (SHIFT) down for the piano to be active:

```
key     ctrl-shift-a     acgrand 400     b1
key     ctrl-shift-z     acgrand 400     c2
key     ctrl-shift-s     acgrand 400     c#2
```

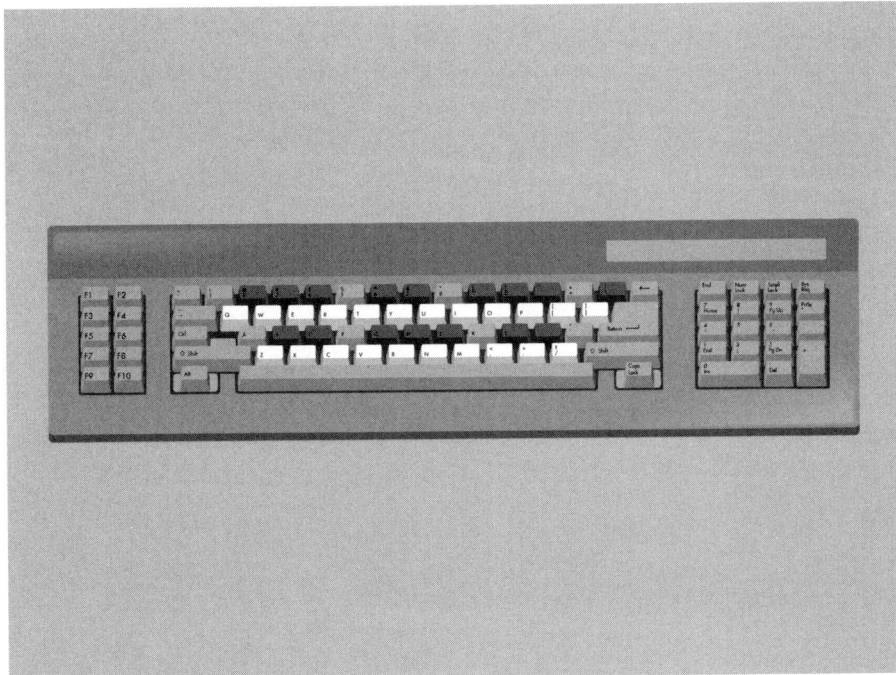

Figure 9-1 Makeshift piano using FMSYS to assign musical tones to keys

(and so on).

If you just wanted a short scale of eight notes, you can use the function keys with ALT like this:

```
alt-f1    acgrand c3
alt-f2    acgrand d3
alt-f3    acgrand e3
```

(and so on for F4 through F8).

CONCLUSION

Begin your day with a rousing fanfare, launch your favorite word processor with a splash, play a quick melody when you're bored, or add haunted house effects to some of those more obscure DOS commands. Use your imagination. There are all sorts of ways of getting DOS to speak up. You can use the tried and true method of batch files to associate any kind of sound with a program, or use FMSYS to assign FM sounds to keystrokes and lots of different DOS events. DOS doesn't have to be silent anymore. And while we would never suggest doing such a thing, it would certainly be possible for some mischievous person to set up a friend's or coworker's machine to make interesting sounds at inopportune times. (Remember, you never read that here.)

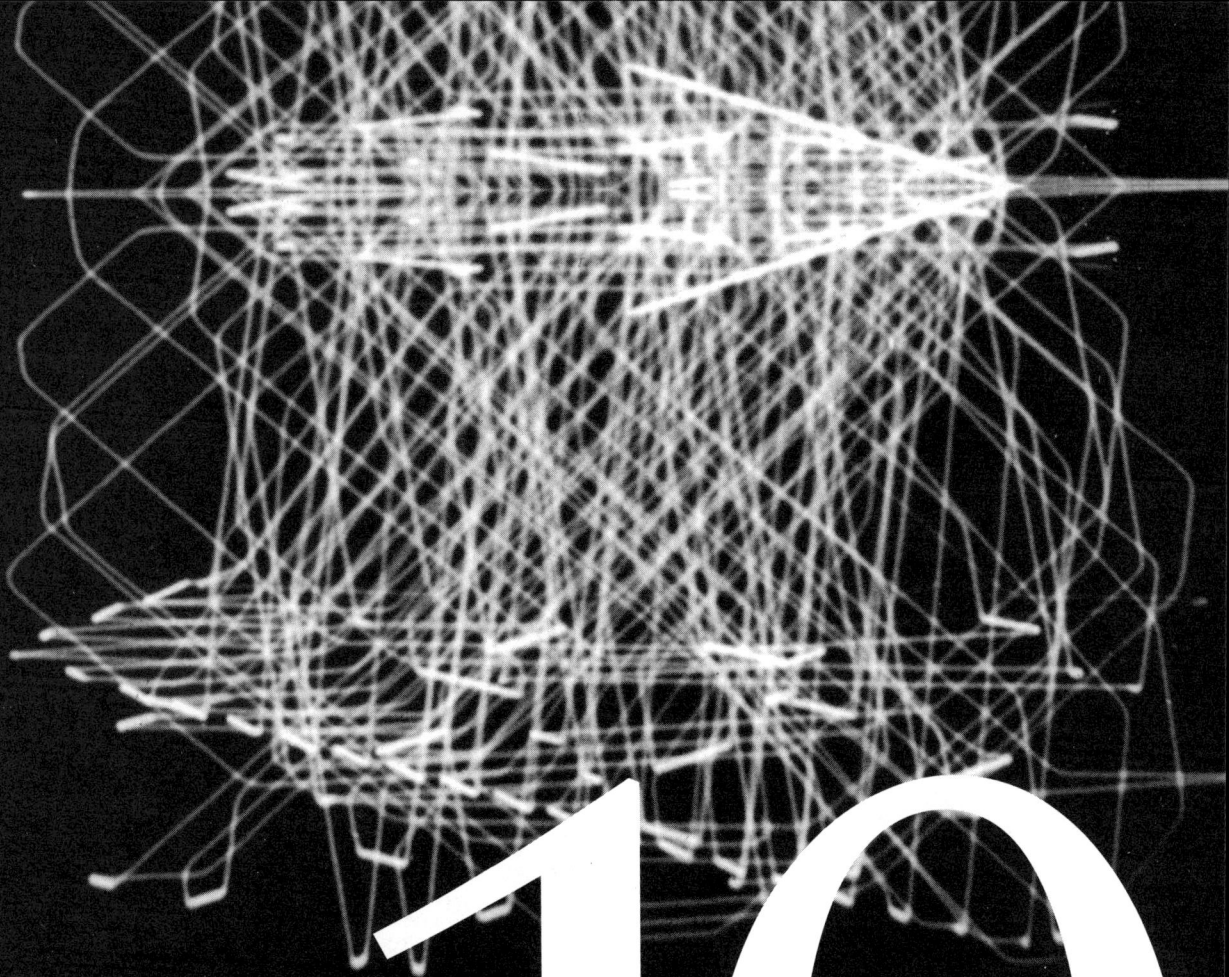

10

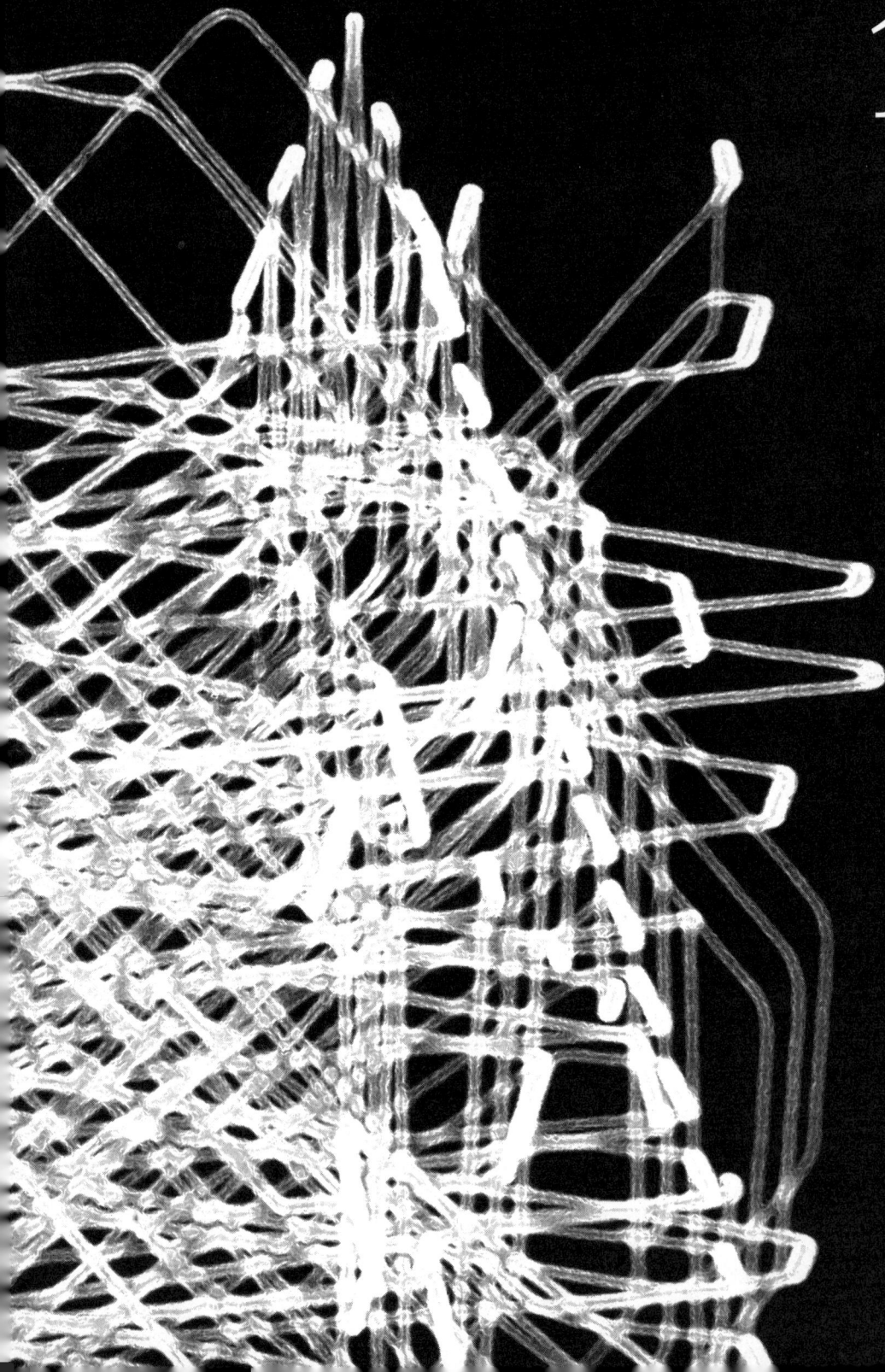

10

Windows Medley

For many years, platforms such as the Macintosh and Amiga held center stage as the systems of choice for multimedia applications. With the add-in capabilities of Multimedia Extensions in Microsoft Windows 3.0, and the addition of Multimedia Extensions as a standard component in version 3.1, Windows has become the new challenger. In fact, support by users and developers has been so great that Windows may be the new leader in the multimedia arena. This chapter takes a look at some of the hot sound features in Windows and covers applications that put them to good use. You'll see how easy it is to listen to sound files, add sounds to everyday Windows functions, create and edit sounds, and use voice recognition for a hands-off approach to Windows.

MULTIMEDIA DEVICES

The term multimedia refers to the whole audio-visual experience, typically meaning the combination of still pictures, animation, video, and audio. Windows tries to treat each of these consistently to make it easy for both

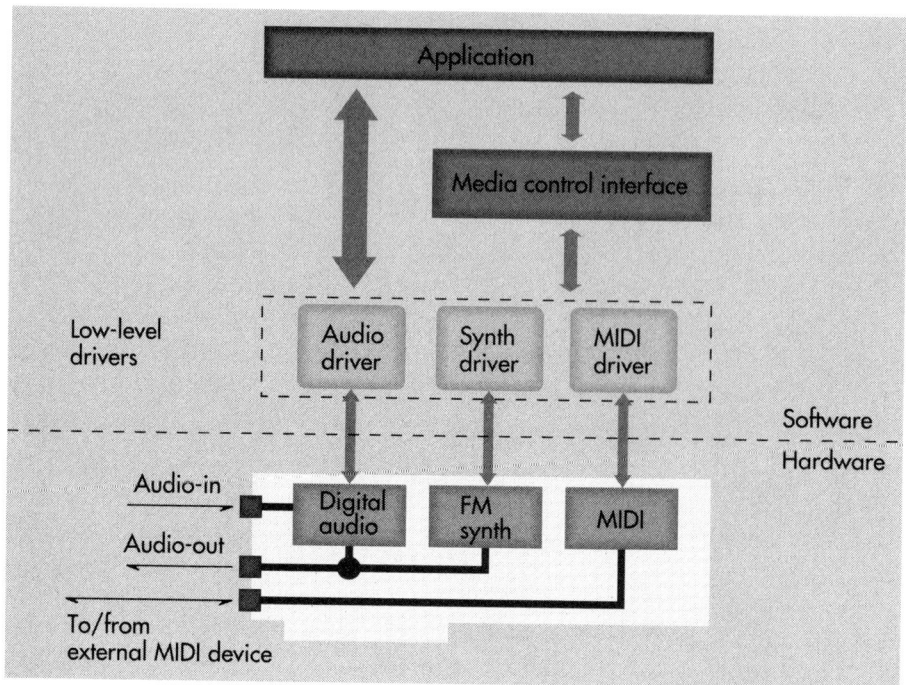

Figure 10-1 Windows talks to a sound card that is actually three devices in one

designers and users to produce and enjoy multimedia presentations. When it works, it works wonderfully well, but when it doesn't, you could be left scratching your head for days. Multimedia support in Windows is built on many layers of software, and if something goes wrong in just one of those layers, you could be sunk. Figure 10-1 shows a conceptual view of a typical sound card and how the different pieces of the system communicate with it.

The diagram in Figure 10-1 points out some of the complexities of getting Windows multimedia devices set up in the first place. The sound card shown is actually three pieces of hardware: (1) an audio I/O section for recording from microphones or other inputs and playing back audio to an amplifier or speaker; (2) a synthesizer section (often FM) for playing music; and (3) a MIDI I/O section for connecting external MIDI devices like keyboard synthesizers. In fact, cards that include a joystick and CD-ROM interface are actually five devices in one.

Each of these specialized hardware sections of the card needs a special software driver that knows how to communicate with it. Those drivers usually

come from the manufacturer of the hardware. The key to Windows' consistency is that no matter how different the underlying hardware, device drivers always (in theory at least) look the same to the applications you are running. That means application designers don't have to worry about all the different kinds of hardware that exist or that might crop up in the future.

To make life easier for developers (and sometimes more complicated for the user), there is something called the Media Control Interface, or MCI. You'll probably come across this term as you're installing applications and drivers. MCI is just another software layer that simulates a typical recording/playback device—anything you might control by pressing Play, Record, Rewind, Pause, and similar buttons. Using this interface, the application only needs to send simple commands to get a job done. For example, to play a song file, the application just gives MCI the name of the file and tells it to start playing. If the application was talking to the low-level driver directly, it would have to get the data from the file, pick it to pieces, and send it out one little bit at a time. The main advantage of MCI is that it lets developers get products to the market much more quickly by building on existing components, but in doing so, they give up some flexibility.

All of these low-level and intermediate types of drivers explain why you see so many entries in the Drivers application in the Control Panel when you install or change the setup for some hardware. Each low-level driver corresponds to a certain type of hardware, even if several types live on the same board. And every MCI driver is there for high-level programming of a particular media type. It's probably a good idea to keep Figure 10-1 handy when you're installing sound hardware, to help clarify things.

THE MEDIA PLAYER

Assuming everything's set up correctly (be sure to follow your hardware installation instructions to the letter), playing any type of sound file is almost too easy: Just start up Windows' standard Media Player program. This application can play MIDI song files (.MID extension), audio files (.WAV extension), tracks on a CD, video clips, or most other types of media you may have installed. The interface always looks the same. Figure 10-2a shows the standard Windows 3.1 Media Player, and 10-2b shows an updated version that began shipping with Video for Windows. Both work pretty much the same. You can usually find the Media Player icon in the Accessories group. Just dou-

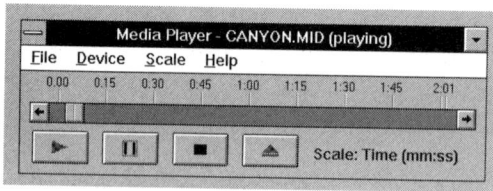

(a) original 3.1 version; (b) replacement version

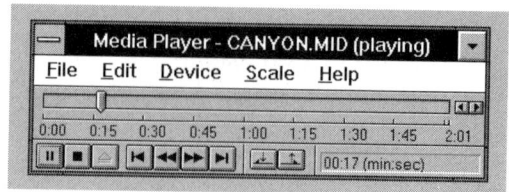

Figure 10-2 Windows' Media Player

ble-click on it to start it up. From the File pull-down menu, locate a sound file you want to play, and once it's loaded, click on the play button (single right arrow). That's all there is to it. The other buttons on the older media player are pause and stop (plus eject for CDs). The newer version has extended controls similar to those on a cassette tape deck or CD player, including buttons for rewind, fast forward, and skip. Both versions have a positioning slider to indicate the current position in the sound file and to let you manually set the position.

Note that for the Media Player and other programs in this chapter, you should be running Windows version 3.1 or higher.

Most of the digitized sound files included with this book are in Sound Blaster VOC format, but the Media Player cannot use them directly. You can, however, convert them to .WAV files for use in Windows. From the DOS prompt, change to the \SEP\VOC directory and type MAKEWAV to automatically create .WAV files from the .VOC files. MAKEWAV is a batch file that runs the SOX program to convert the included .VOC files. Be sure you have at least as much disk space available as the space the .VOC files occupy (about half a megabyte). You can also use SOX to convert files individually (see Appendix A), or you may use the Blaster Master program to load .VOC files and convert (export) them to .WAV files.

ATTACHING SOUNDS IN WINDOWS

Because of the more logical and consistent design of Windows, attaching sounds to programs and events is much simpler than in DOS. To see how this works, we'll try out a shareware program called Whoop It Up!, written by

Steven Schauer and published by Starlite Software. Whoop It Up! resides in the \SEP\WHP directory. To run it, select Run... from the File menu in the Windows Program Manager. Type \SEP\WHP\WHOOP and press (ENTER). You'll first see an introductory screen explaining that this version of Whoop It Up! is for evaluation only, and how to acquire a licensed copy. If you agree to the terms, click on I Agree to continue. The Whoop It Up! control panel appears, as in Figure 10-3.

In Windows, just about everything that happens is an event, and we can intercept and assign sounds to most of them. Take note of the three buttons on the right of the Whoop It Up! window that select the classes of events we can change: System Events, Generic Events, and Application. System Events are normal Windows functions that aren't related to specific applications. Starting up, shutting down, and error or information pop-ups are examples. Clicking on System Events displays those possible events in the list box in the upper left part of the Whoop It Up! window.

When you click a particular item in the Event list, the sound file associated with that event (if any) gets highlighted in the list below. To change the associated sound, just click on another sound file. Scrolling to the bottom of the list, you can change to other drives and directories to use any other files you might have. By default, you see the sound files included with Whoop It Up!. Any .WAV or .MID file is a valid sound file to use. If you double-click on the

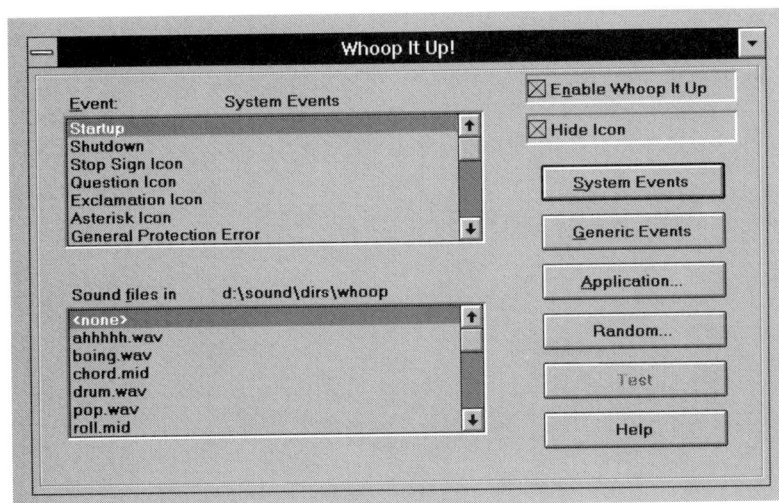

Figure 10-3 Whoop It Up!'s control panel showing sounds being attached to system events

133

sound file name, Whoop It Up! plays it for you. You can also click on Test to play the selected file. To remove an association, click on the <none> entry at the top of the list.

If you click the Generic Events button, you'll see a new set of events that typically apply to a running Windows program, such as starting, stopping, maximizing, and minimizing. The term "generic" refers to the fact that the associated sounds apply to these events in all programs. To associate certain sounds with events in applications you choose, use the Application... button. In this demo version, the only program you can set up is the Note Pad, but in the licensed version, you can customize any number of programs with special sounds. Also available in the full version is the Random... function, which shuffles sounds randomly among events.

That's about all there is to setting up sounds. Whoop It Up! is one of those few programs that does a lot, but remains simple and clean in its design. Minimize Whoop It Up! to keep the sounds you defined in effect—don't close it. To have it automatically start up each time you run Windows, add a program item to the Windows Startup group using the Program Manager File menu. Give the full path name, as we did to run it directly (\SEP\WHP\WHOOP).

SOUND RECORDER

Windows ships with a handy application called Sound Recorder. Not only can it record sounds and produce .WAV files, but it's also useful for playing them back. Figure 10-4 shows Sound Recorder in action. Its control buttons are

Figure 10-4 Windows' Sound Recorder showing a recorded waveform

similar to Media Player's, and for playing back sounds, you can use either program interchangeably. One obvious difference, though, is the animated waveform display in Sound Recorder. It works very much like the sound scopes we saw in earlier chapters. Because the display area is rather small, you can't see much detail, but it is useful for rough positioning in the sound clip.

Try recording something and you'll see how the program works. The Sound Recorder icon should be in the Accessories group; double-click on it to start it up. Then click the record (microphone) button on the right to begin recording. Click the stop button when you're done (the button with the square to the left of record). That's all there is to it. Click the rewind button (double left arrow) and then play (single right arrow) to listen to your recording. If you're happy with it, select Save from the File menu to save your recording as a .WAV file.

Sound Recorder can also do simple editing. If you change the position of the slider to a particular point in the sound clip (the position in hundredths of a second appears on the left), you can insert or mix another sound file at that point. The Insert-File and Mix-with-File functions are found on the Edit pull-down menu. Use Insert to add another file at the current point, pushing back any original material to make room. Use Mix to add the new file on top of the old material to hear both at once. This is not as precise as using a full-blown sound editor, but it's often useful for quick-and-dirty editing.

There are also some handy sound processing functions on the Effects menu. You can increase or decrease the volume, double or halve the speed, add echo, or reverse the sample. There is a lot more to this application than first meets the eye. If you need additional recording and editing capabilities in Windows, you'll want to look into programs like Wave Editor discussed in the next section. Also, see Appendix C for other sources of sound editing software.

DIGITAL EDITING

Although Sound Recorder can handle some simple sound editing tasks, to do any serious editing in Windows of the kind we did with Blaster Master, you'll need a more capable application. In this section we'll look briefly at one commercial program called Wave Editor, written by Keith Boone. The Wave Editor demo we've included is another shareware program published by Starlite Software (who also brought you Whoop It Up!). To start Wave Editor, select Run... from the Program Manager's File menu and type

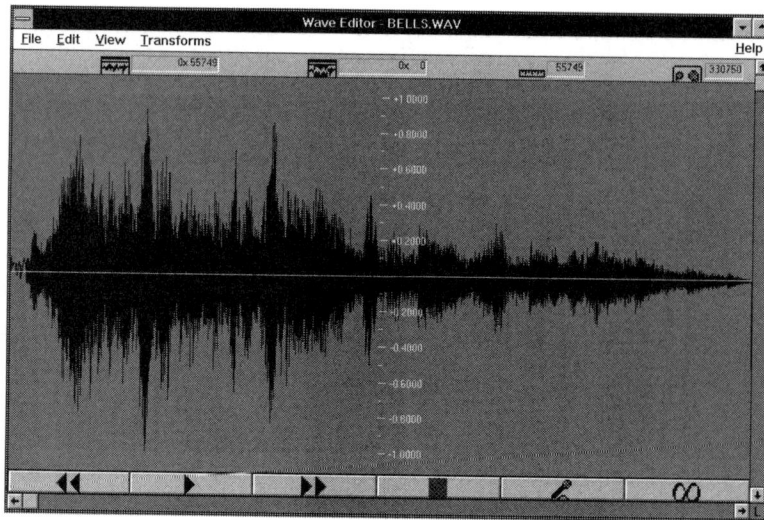

Figure 10-5 Wave Editor's display showing an existing sound file

\SEP\WEDIT\WAVEEDIT. You'll see a startup screen explaining usage terms and how to acquire a licensed version of the program. After you've read this information, click on OK to continue. The Wave Editor window with a sound file already loaded appears, as shown in Figure 10-5.

The controls and menus in Wave Editor are straightforward and consistent with other types of Windows applications. The control buttons at the bottom are almost identical to Sound Recorder's, with the addition of a loop button (infinity sign), which plays a selected sound repeatedly until you press the stop button. The File menu contains familiar operations such as New, Open, and Save, plus some configuration options. To load a file, select Open, locate a .WAV file you want to work with, and click on it. Wave Editor displays the sound's waveform, and all you need to do is click the play button to hear it.

Selecting portions of the sound for editing is just like selecting text in other Windows programs: Click your mouse on the waveform at the beginning of a section of sound, and while holding the mouse button down, move the cursor to the end of that section. The colors of the selected section are reversed so that you can see it more easily. To pick another section, click at the beginning of the new section and drag the cursor to the end.

After you've selected a section, normal Windows editing functions are available from the Edit menu. You can remove the selection and copy it to the Clipboard with Cut, make a Clipboard copy without removing it using Copy,

136

remove it entirely with Delete, and of course, if you make a mistake, Undo the last edit. Some handy new edit functions include Duplicate Selection, for inserting a copy of the selection right after itself; Erase Selection, to remove the section leaving a silent space; and Insert Silence, to fill the selected region with silence and push back the existing material.

To examine a selection more closely, click on the Zoom In item on the View menu. This magnifies the selection so that it fills the whole width of the window. While zoomed in, you can use the horizontal scroll bar at the bottom of the window to move around and view different parts of the waveform. To change the size of the zoomed area, use the vertical scroll bar on the right side of the window. Moving down zooms in, while moving up zooms out.

You'll find some of Wave Editor's most useful and interesting features on the Transforms menu. The first item, Fourier, performs various mathematical transformations on the data. The Fourier transform, you may recall, was the basis for the frequency analysis plots we looked at in earlier chapters. These functions actually change your data, so be sure not to save the results if you want to keep the original (or save them under a different name). If you're not mathematically inclined, you may still want to try a series of different transforms on your sample, because although multiple transforms may not be meaningful, you may get some interesting *sounding* results if you play them. The Filters option on the Transforms menu is not completely enabled in this demo version. Other functions include Echo, Volume, and Reverse, which you're already familiar with from corresponding functions in Blaster Master.

VOICE RECOGNITION

Controlling your computer using voice commands is one of the hottest new sound application areas. Chapter 4 discussed some of the basics of computers and speech. Here we'll look at a demo of a superb voice recognition package from Command Corp. called IN3 (pronounced "in-cube"). Just as we attached sounds to Windows functions earlier, IN3 lets you assign voice commands to most Windows functions so you can perform those functions by speaking into a microphone.

Command Corp. states that IN3 works best on faster processors with higher-resolution sound cards. While it does need at least a 386 processor, recognition will still be very good using lower-quality sound cards. To start the demo, select Run... from the Program Manager's File menu and type \SEP\IN3\IN3DEMO. The main IN3 window pops up, as shown in Figure 10-6.

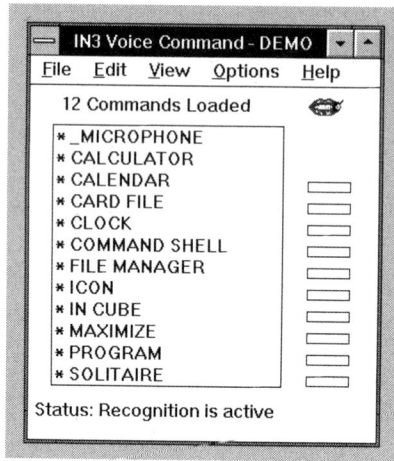

Figure 10-6 IN3's main window showing commands available in the demo

The dozen words listed are the functions the demo version supports. IN3 is a speaker-dependent recognition system, so you must train it with your own voice to recognize these words. Select Build Template on the Edit menu to start the training process. On the Build Template dialog, select Create and All, and then click Begin. IN3 will show you each word in order, asking you to say it twice. Then it will make a test pass through all the words to make sure it understands you when you say them. It's a quick, painless process that takes just a few moments. You should try to be reasonably consistent in your speech, but it's not necessary to speak with robotlike precision; the recognizer is very flexible.

When you're finished with the training, IN3 becomes active, and you can start speaking commands. Some of the commands, such as Calendar, Clock, and Card File, correspond to standard Windows programs. Just say their names to start them. Other commands are generic functions (such as Icon and Maximize) and apply to the currently active window. Once you've become accustomed to the commands, you can reduce IN3 to an icon and ignore it. It will keep listening for your commands and act on them when it hears something it recognizes. Being a continuous speech recognizer, it will even pick words out of sentences. For example, you could say, "I'd like a clock now please," and voilà, you get a clock!

Although you can't add any commands in the demo version, you can see how commands and Windows functions are associated using the New Command option on the Edit menu. You can associate keystroke sequences, programs, and other functions with the command. Click Help for information on setting up new commands and for details on other IN3 functions. Be sure to check the README file in \SEP\IN3 for system requirements, ordering information, and further usage instructions.

CONCLUSION

With all the different types of hardware available, Windows multimedia can be bewildering. Just getting the drivers straight is sometimes a real challenge. However, because of the consistency of Windows multimedia software design, everything should be smooth sailing once the drivers are installed and set up. Applications can concentrate on getting the job done, rather than worrying about the hardware. And because of consistent behavior among devices and software, it's simple to use programs like Whoop It Up! to modify the basic system behavior and assign sounds to events. If you've struggled with this in DOS, you'll find Windows quite a relief.

Built-in applications like Media Player and Sound Recorder point out how well-integrated sound has become in Windows. In fact, just clicking on a sound file in the File Manager will play it, using the correct application. Although only the bare minimum in tools comes standard, the underlying structure makes it possible to add a wide variety of third-party applications that present a very comprehensive collection of capabilities.

Shareware Notice

Whoop It Up! and Wave Editor have been generously provided by Starlite Software to help present key concepts in this book. These are shareware programs, however, so if you like them and continue to use them, you are required to purchase registered copies. Both programs are distributed in the United States by:

Advanced Support Group
11900 Grant Pl.
Des Peres, MO 63131
Orders only: (800) 767-9611
Information & registered users technical support: (314) 965-5630

Worldwide distribution is by:
Starlite Software Co.
P.O. Box 370
Hadlock, WA 98339
(206) 437-0116
CompuServe: 71431,1571

See the file ORDER.TXT in \SEP\WHP and \SEP\WEDIT for detailed ordering information.

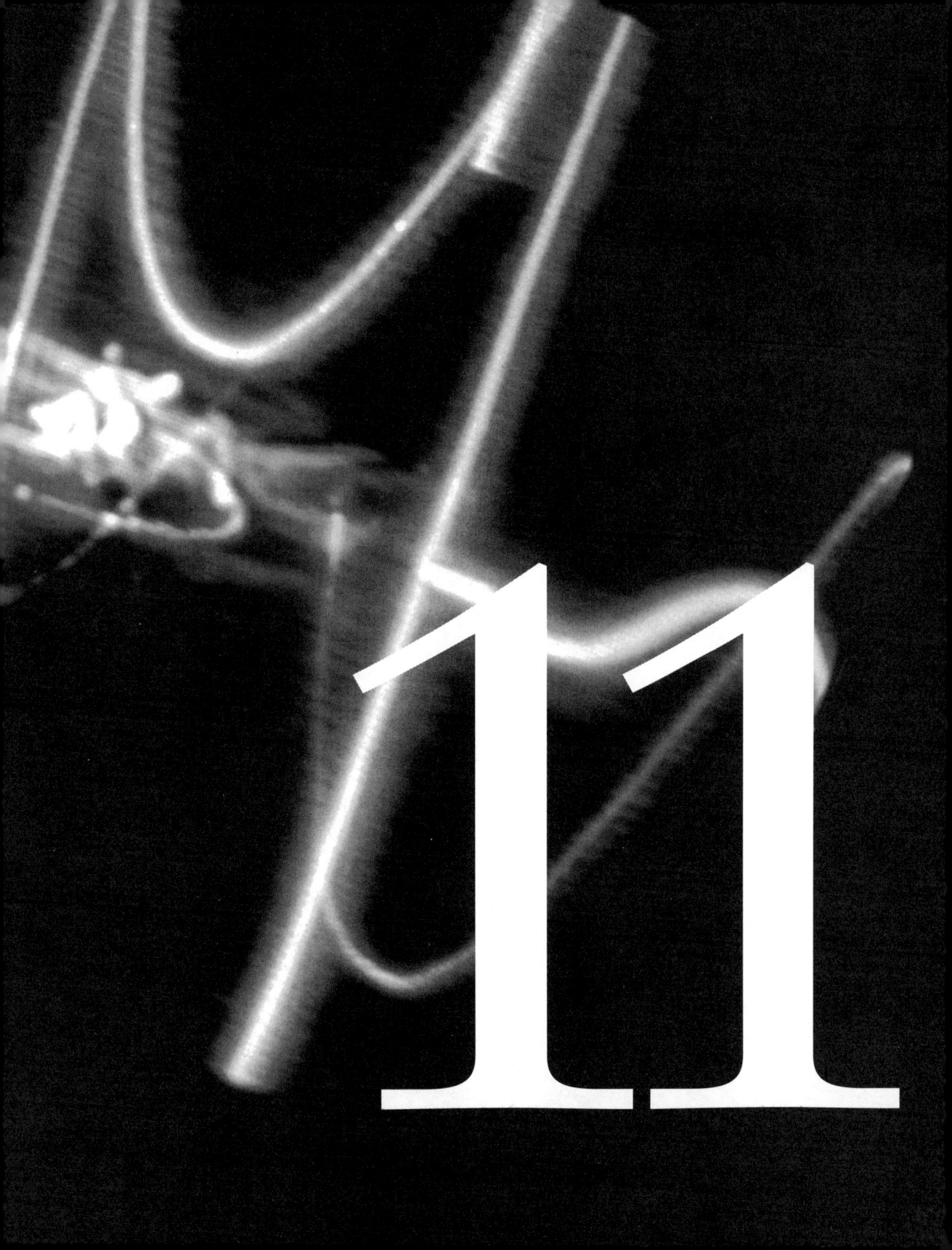

11

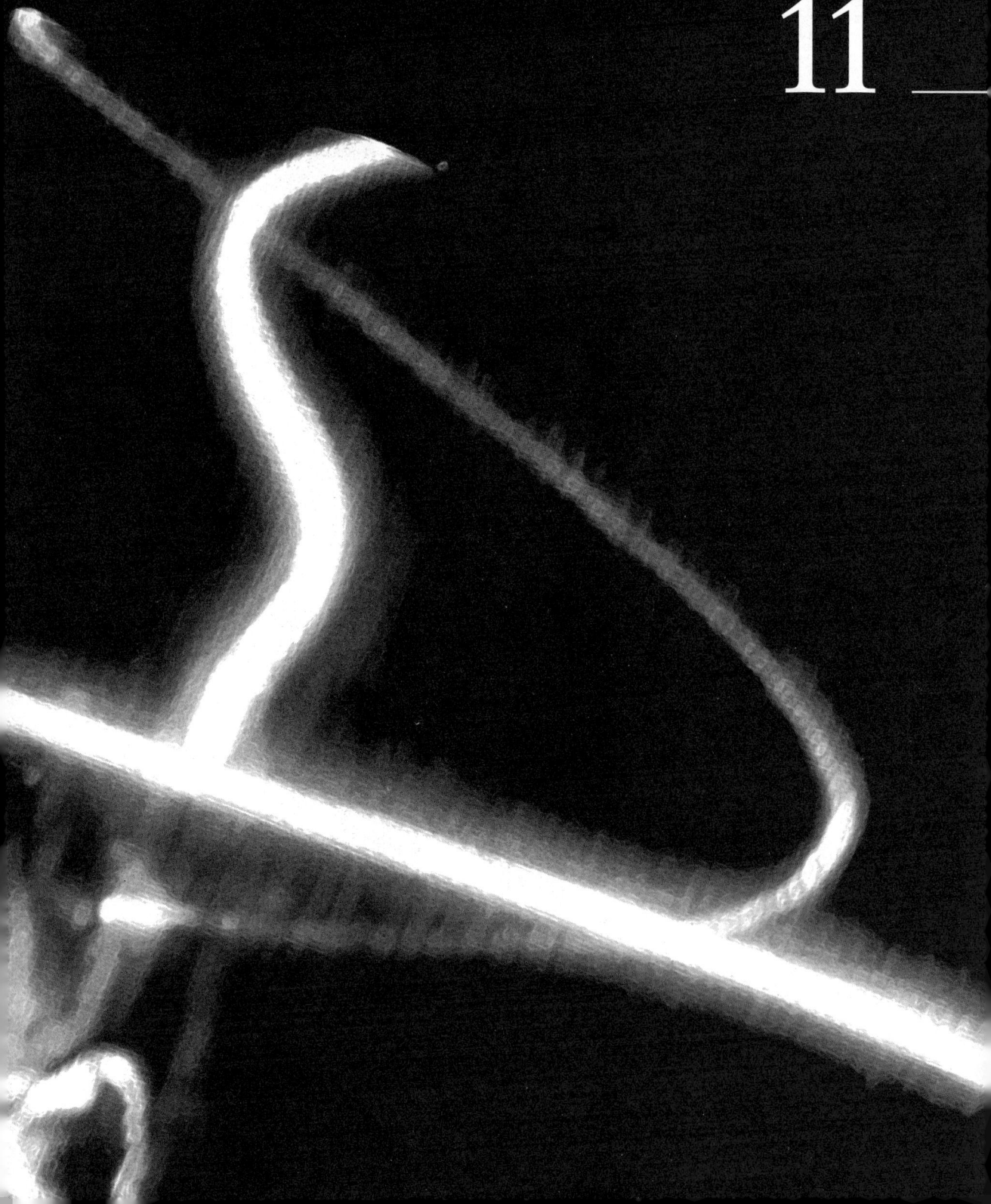

Taking Inventory

We've covered enough different programs, data file formats, and techniques by now that your head may be spinning. This chapter is dedicated to helping sort it all out—answering the question, "Where was that program?" The type of file or program is grouped by topic area to aid you in locating material in the other chapters, and among the megabytes of files that accompany this book. Chances are, you'll want to go back and try something out that caught your fancy. Here's where to start looking.

DIGITIZED SOUND

Digitally sampled sounds come in a variety of file formats, but we only talked about .VOC and .WAV files. A collection of .VOC files accompanies this book, along with a set of 3-D sound files in Windows WAV format. The locations of the various files and players and editors for them are summarized in Table 11-1.

File Type	Directory	File Name	Chapter
Sound Blaster voice files	\SEP\VOC	*.VOC	2, 3, 9
VOC players	\SEP\BMSTR	BMASTER.EXE	2, 3
	\SEP\VOC	PLAYVOC.EXE	9
3-D sound files	\SEP\QSOUND	*.WAV	5
WAV editors (DOS)	\SEP\BMSTR	BMASTER.EXE	2
WAV editors (Windows)	Sound Recorder in Accessories group		10
	\SEP\WEDIT	WAVEEDIT.EXE	10
WAV players (Windows)	Media Player in Accessories group		10
Sampling rate demo	\SEP\SOUND	RDEMO.BAT	1
Bit resolution demo	\SEP\SOUND	BDEMO.BAT	1
Converting VOC to WAV	\SEP\VOC	MAKEWAV.BAT	10

Table 11-1 Digitized sound files, players, and editors

MUSIC

We discussed song files in Standard MIDI and Mod format. A number of songs in these formats are included with this book. Standard MIDI is the most common format for song interchange, and mod files, having their roots in song players for the Amiga, contain their own sampled sound data. Table 11-2 summarizes the available files and players.

144

File Type	Directory	File Name	Chapter
Standard MIDI song files	\SEP\MIDI	*.MID	7, 9, 10
Batch MIDI player (DOS)	\SEP\MIDI	PLAYB.EXE	7, 9
Background MIDI player (DOS)	\SEP\MIDI	PLAYR.EXE	7
MIDI player (Windows)	Media Player in Accessories group		10
Mod files	\SEP\MOD	*.MOD	8
Mod file players	\SEP\MOD	RUNDMP.BAT	8
		RUNPMP.BAT	8

Table 11-2 Song files and players

FM SOUNDS

FM sounds are most often used for making music, but they can also be used for creating interesting sound effects. Table 11-3 summarizes the types of FM files included, plus the utility programs we used to work with them.

File Type	Directory	File Name	Chapter
FM sound banks (128 sounds)	\SEP\FM	*.IBK	6
Single FM sounds	\SEP\FM	*.SBI	9
FM sound editor	\SEP\FM	SBTIMBRE.EXE	6
FM sound player (for SBI)	\SEP\FM	PLAYFM.EXE	9
Resident FM sound player	\SEP\FM	FMSYS.EXE	9
FM demos	\SEP\FM	*.BAT	6

Table 11-3 FM sounds and utilities

SOUND ANALYSIS PROGRAMS

We used several different programs for viewing sounds and extracting various types of information from them. These programs are summarized in Table 11-4.

Program Type	Directory	File Name	Chapter
Real-time waveform display	\SEP\SOUND	ASCOPE.EXE	1
	\SEP\BMSTR	BMASTER.EXE	2, 3
Real-time frequency display	\SEP\SOUND	MF.BAT	1
Waveform viewing (DOS)	\SEP\BMSTR	BMASTER.EXE	2, 3
Waveform viewing (Windows)	\SEP\WEDIT	WAVEEDIT.EXE	10

Table 11-4 Sound analysis programs

SPEECH RECOGNITION

We talked about how individual words and phrases could be analyzed and visually examined some of their characteristics. Then we looked at speech recognition both in the form of a simple defense game and as a real productivity aid. Table 11-5 lists these programs and their locations.

Program Type	Directory	File Name	Chapter
Voice command game	\SEP\SOUND	VDEMO.EXE	4
Speech viewing	\SEP\SOUND	WSCOPE.EXE	4
Real-time frequency display	\SEP\SOUND	MF.BAT	4
Windows command recognition	\SEP\IN3	IN3DEMO.EXE	10

Table 11-5 Speech programs

ATTACHING SOUNDS

Livening up normal computer activities with sound was a topic of discussion for both DOS and Windows. Table 11-6 summarizes the techniques and programs we used to do this.

Technique / Program	Directory	File Name	Chapter
Batch files (DOS)			9
VOC player	\SEP\VOC	PLAYVOC.EXE	9
FM sound player	\SEP\FM	PLAYFM.EXE	9
Batch MIDI player	\SEP\MIDI	PLAYB.EXE	7, 9
FM sound attachment (DOS)	\SEP\FM	FMSYS.EXE	9
Sound attachment (Windows)	\SEP\WHP	WHOOP.EXE	10

Table 11-6 Attaching sounds

DIRECTORIES

If you installed the programs and data according to the installation instructions, you should have a \SEP directory containing a number of subdirectories. Table 11-7 summarizes the subdirectories, their contents, and the chapters using them.

\SEP Subdirectory	Contents	Chapter
BMSTR	Blaster Master program and samples	2, 3
FM	SBTimbre, PlayFM, FMSYS, FM sounds	6, 9
IN3	IN3 voice recognition demo (Windows)	10
MIDI	Play/B, Play/R, MIDI files	7, 9
MOD	DMP, PMP, mod files	8
QSOUND	3-D sound demo files	5
SOUND	ASCOPE, MicFFT, WSCOPE, voice game	1, 4
VOC	PlayVOC, VOC sound files	9
WEDIT	Wave Editor (Windows)	10
WHP	Whoop It Up! (Windows)	10

Table 11-7 *Sound Effects Playhouse* directories

A FINAL WORD

We hope you have found this book to be both enjoyable and educational. We've covered a lot of ground, but only just scratched the surface of the remarkable world of sound. We've tried to include a large enough assortment of tools, toys, and sample sounds to keep you occupied for a long time. If you find this material tantalizing, by all means go out and look for more of the same. The appendixes list a number of great sources for sounds and software.

You'll find that using sound in your everyday computing activities eventually becomes second nature, and you'll wonder how you ever got along without it. And if sound as an end product is your main interest, you'll discover that computers simplify the process of sound and music production immensely. You should be in a better position now to evaluate what you need and what's available, so go to it. Have fun, and don't forget that dogs hear higher pitches than we do, so be kind to the neighborhood pets!

APPENDIX A

Sound Formats and Conversion

Nearly every computer platform has at least one unique format for representing sounds; some use several. The sound files you want to use with a particular application are likely to come in a variety of formats. Listed below are some of the more common formats. You can convert among all of them using the included SOX program, written by Lance Norskog and other contributors.

VOC: CREATIVE LABS VOICE FORMAT

These 8-bit files are most commonly used with Sound Blaster and compatible PC sound cards. They may contain stereo, looping, and compression information, though not all players will handle anything beyond basic monophonic sound data.

WAV: MICROSOFT WAVE FORMAT

Wave files are the standard sound file format used in Microsoft Windows. Increasingly, DOS programs are supporting the format because it has become so widespread. Wave format is a subset of the Microsoft RIFF multimedia file format specification. It is able to represent a wide range of sound resolutions, sampling rates, compression, and other special information. Most Windows applications expect mono or stereo files using 8 or 16 bits and a sampling rate of 11.025 kHz, 22.05 kHz, or 44.1 kHz. Some applications and sound cards now support Microsoft's ADPCM compression standard, which can reduce 16-bit sound (with some loss) to 25 percent of the original size.

AIFF: APPLE II AUDIO FORMAT

The AIFF format was developed by Apple to represent various types of multimedia data. You will be able to convert these files to another sound format if they only contain audio data (an AIFF file containing picture data would not be usable). The AIFF format is also a standard sound file format on Silicon Graphics workstations.

AU: SUN AUDIO FORMAT

Although there are several (incompatible) variants of the AU format, audio files originating on Sun workstations will be primarily in this format and can be converted without difficulty. DEC and NeXT also use AU format, but with additions that may not convert properly.

RAW: UNFORMATTED SOUND DATA

There are a number of raw audio formats. "Raw" means that there is nothing but sound data in the file—no headers or other information that might tell you what the file contains or how it is to be used. Such files must be accompa-

nied by a description of the data in order to use them without a lot of trial and error. The kinds of information you need to know are the number of bits (8 or 16), whether the data is signed or unsigned, the sampling rate, and whether compression was used. If this information isn't provided, you'll have to guess.

USING SOX TO CONVERT SOUND FILES

The SOX program is a powerful, no-frills conversion utility. You can find it in the \SEP\VOC directory. It runs from the DOS command line and uses various command line options to direct its operation. It also supports a small set of sound effects (such as echo and filtering) that you can apply during conversion. Fortunately, most readers of this book will be dealing with the more common PC formats (WAV and VOC), which simplifies command line usage. If you give the correct extension for the input and output files, SOX will know what type of conversion to do. So to convert from FROGS.VOC to FROGS.WAV, just type

```
sox frogs.voc frogs.wav (ENTER)
```

No options are necessary in this case because you're not changing anything but the overall format. Without the file extensions, you would have to specify the files and formats in the following order:

```
sox input_options input_file output_options output_file
```

To convert a file called STRANGE, which is raw, 8-bit, unsigned, and recorded at 22,050 Hz, to a WAV file called NEW.WAV having a sampling rate of 11,025 Hz, you'd type the following:

```
sox -t .ub -r 22050 strange -r 11025 new.wav (ENTER)
```

The most common file format options are listed in Table A-1. Note that the case of the option letters is significant. For example, -u and -U are two different options, so don't capitalize letters unless you mean it.

You can add effects options such as "echo" to the end of the SOX command line. Some of these effects are listed in Table A-2. To add echo to a file, BIRD.WAV, creating CAVEBIRD.WAV, you would type

```
sox bird.wav cavebird.wav echo (ENTER)
```

151

Option	Description
-t file type	File type if there is no file extension. Some common types supported by SOX:
	.voc Creative Labs voice
	.wav Microsoft wave
	.aiff Apple II audio
	.au Sun audio
	.sf IRCAM audio
	.smp Turtle Beach SampleVision format
	.raw No header information
	.ub Raw: unsigned byte (8-bit)
	.sb Raw: signed byte
	.uw Raw: unsigned word (16-bit)
	.sw Raw: signed word
	.ul Raw: uLaw encoded byte
-r sample rate	Sampling rate in Hz (samples per second); 8000 is assumed if this option is not given and there is no header
-s	Data is signed
-u	Data is unsigned
-b	Byte data (8-bit)
-w	Word data (16-bit)
-c channels	Number of channels: 1 (mono), 2 (stereo), 4 (quad)

Additional file types and options can be found in the file \SEP\VOC\SOX.TXT.

Table A-1 Common SOX formatting options

Filters are very important in audio processing. Three common types that SOX supports are Low Pass, Band Pass, and High Pass filters. Filters remove or reduce certain frequencies that make up sound. A low pass filter retains low frequencies, and removes high frequencies. If you have a sound sample with a lot of hissing background noise, you may be able to reduce the hissing (which is mostly high frequency noise) using a low pass filter. Figure A-1 shows how these three types of filters affect the same sound. The first graph represents the original frequency components in the sound, and the others show what happens using the different filters. The grayed areas show the frequencies least affected by the filters.

Option	Description
echo [delay volume]	Applies echo giving optional delay in seconds and volume between 0 and 1; for example: echo 0.1 0.5
vibro speed [depth]	Adds vibrato-type effect. Speed is a frequency less than 30, and the optional depth is a number from 0 to 1 (default 0.5)
lowp [center]	Applies low pass filter with an optional cutoff frequency (center)
highp [center]	Applies high pass filter with an optional cutoff frequency
bandp center [width]	Applies a band pass filter at the given center frequency and optional width
reverse	Reverses the entire sound file

See the file \SEP\VOC\SOX.TXT for more information on SOX effects.

Table A-2 Common SOX effects options

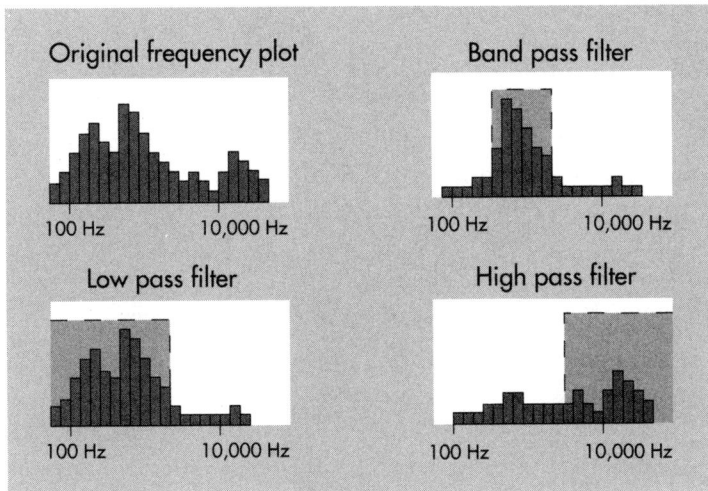

Figure A-1 Types of sound filters available in SOX

153

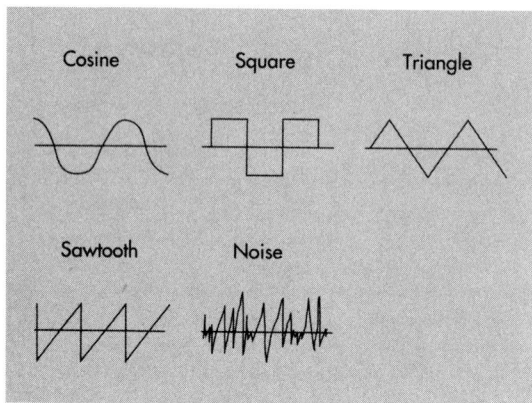

Figure A-2 Types of waveforms that can be used to create new sounds in Wave Editor

Following are some effects examples:
Add echo with delay of 3 tenths of a second at 20 percent volume.

```
sox bird.wav cavebird.wav echo 0.3 0.2
```

Reduce high-frequency information.

```
sox bird.wav lowbird.wav lowp
```

Reduce frequencies above 10 kHz.

```
sox bird.wav bird1.wav lowp 10000
```

Emphasize frequencies near 2 kHz.

```
sox bird.wav twtybird.wav bandp 2000
```

SOX is a public domain program, and enhancements are welcomed by the author. You can obtain the complete SOX distribution, including C source code, on CompuServe in MIDIFORUM, or via the Internet at wuarchive.wustl.edu and other sites (see Appendix B). Search for the key word "sox," or file names containing the letters "sox" (file names are subject to change with new releases and according to site preferences).

B

Sound and Music Sources

PUBLIC DOMAIN FILES

Public domain sound and music files are available through numerous online sources. Most of these sources also include a wide variety of public domain and shareware programs.

CompuServe Information Service

CompuServe contains the most comprehensive collection of sound and music files, software, information, and vendor support facilities of any online service. Look in the following special interest group forums for sound-related material.

Mod files

Amiga Arts forum (go amigaarts)
Multimedia Vendor forum (go multiven)

MIDI and Sound Files

MIDI/Music forums (go midi)
IBM New User forum (go ibmnew)
Multimedia forum (go multimedia)

For CompuServe membership information, call
U.S. and Canada   (800) 848-8199
Other countries (+1) 614-457-0802

Or write to the following address:
CompuServe
5000 Arlington Centre Blvd.
Columbus, OH 43220

Internet FTP Sites

The Internet is a vast collection of high-speed national and regional networks connecting thousands of schools, research institutions, and businesses. Internet sites contain a wealth of sound files and software, and some of the best locations are listed here. If you have Internet access through your school or company, use your local ftp (file transfer protocol) facility to make anonymous ftp connections to any of these sites. If you need assistance, contact your system administrator or pick up one of several good introductory books available on using the Internet.

Internet Sites

---

ftp.cica.indiana.edu
oak.oakland.edu
saffron.inset.com
ucsd.edu
wuarchive.wustl.edu
snake.mcs.kent.edu

Bulletin Board Systems (Sound/Music/Software)

Independently operated bulletin board systems can be found in most areas of the United States and internationally. Three of the largest and best-stocked music and sound bulletin boards in the United States are listed here. Note that there may be membership fees or contributions required for full access to all message and data areas.

Eastern United States

ENIAC
Rockville, MD
Modem: (301) 460-9134

Central United States

Sound Management
Chicago, IL
Modem: (708) 949-6434

Western United States

MIDI and Multimedia Exchange
San Francisco, CA
Modem: (415) 771-1788

COMMERCIAL SOURCES

The following companies have thousands of sound and music files available on diskette and CD-ROM. The types of files they specialize in—sound (.VOC, .WAV, and so on), music (MIDI files), or both—are listed on the left.

Type of File	Company
Sound	Sound Source Unlimited 2985 E. Hillcrest Drive, Suite A Westlake Village, CA 91362 (805) 494-9996
Sound and Music	PROSONUS 11126 Weddington North Hollywood, CA 91601 (818) 766-5221
Music	Tran Tracks 350 5th Avenue #3304 New York, NY 10118 (201) 383-6691
Music	Trycho Tunes 2166 W. Broadway St., Suite 330 Anaheim, CA 92804 (800) 543-8988
Music	Romeo Music 214 Lincoln St., Suite 104 Allston, MA 02134 (800) 852-2122
Sound	The Music Factory P.O. Box 1089 Saugus, MA 01906 (617) 595-0684
Production mod music for games and other commercial applications	Jim Young U4ic Productions 32 Ingleside Rd. Kingswood, Bristol BS15 1HQ U.K. 011-44-272-613792

Software Suppliers

VOICE RECOGNITION SOFTWARE

These voice recognition packages let you control your system through spoken words. You can add hundreds of commands to assist in program control, data entry, and editing. They are all reasonably priced and work with popular sound cards.

IN3 (Windows; speaker-dependent)
  Command Corp.
  3675 Crestwood Parkway
  Duluth, GA 30136
  (404) 925-7950

IBM VoiceType Control (Windows; speaker-independent)
  Available through IBM retail channels.
  Developed by:
  Dragon Systems
  320 Nevada Street
  Newton, MA 02160
  (617) 965-5200

Voice Blaster (DOS and Windows; speaker-dependent)
Covox
675 Conger St.
Eugene, OR 97402
(503) 342-1271

MUSIC SEQUENCERS

If you like to create your own music, or just need to fix up songs you have acquired from other sources, you'll need a music sequencer. These programs are the word processors of music. They let you record live music from a MIDI keyboard, layer multiple tracks of music, make corrections, and even enter music using your mouse or computer keyboard. Some use displays resembling piano rolls for entry and editing, and others use standard music notation. There is a wide range of products from which to choose. The ones listed represent some of the best and most popular packages, ranging in price from under $100 to several hundred dollars, depending on the capabilities you need. Some vendors provide entry level as well as professional sequencing packages.

Cakewalk (DOS and Windows versions)
Twelve Tone Systems
P.O. Box 760
Watertown, MA 02272
(800) 243-1171 or (617) 273-4437

WinJammer (Windows); available as shareware on many online services
Dan McKee
WinJammer Software Ltd.
69 Rancliffe Road
Oakville, Ontario
Canada L6H 1B1

Sequencer Plus (DOS and Windows versions)
Voyetra Technologies
5 Odell Plaza
Yonkers, NY 10701-1406
(914) 966-0600

Cadenza (DOS and Windows versions)
  Big Noise Software
  P.O. Box 23740
  Jacksonville, FL 32241
  (904) 730-0754

Studio, Recording Session (Windows)
  Midisoft
  P.O. Box 1000
  Bellevue, WA 98009
  (206) 881-7176

Master Tracks Pro (Windows)
  Passport Designs
  100 Stone Pine Rd.
  Half Moon Bay, CA 94019
  (415) 726-0280

Ballade (DOS and Windows versions)
  DYNAWARE USA
  950 Tower Lane, Suite 1150
  Foster City, CA 94404
  (415) 349-5700

DIGITAL AUDIO TOOLS

When working with digital audio, the tools you use are very important in assuring good sound quality. Digital sound recording and editing tools have become quite sophisticated in their capabilities, but still reduce common operations to simple steps very much like those you would follow in a word processor. Although some of these packages are regularly used in professional audio applications, they are priced within reach of the home user.

Blaster Master (DOS; see Chapter 2)
  Gary Maddox
  1901 Spring Creek #315
  Plano, TX 75023

Wave for Windows, Turtle Tools (Windows)
  Turtle Beach Systems
  52 Grumbacher Road
  York, PA 17402
  (800) 645-5640

Sound Professional (Windows)
  Digital Soup
  P.O. Box 1340
  Brattleboro, VT 05302
  (800) 793-7356 or (802) 254-7356

AudioView (Windows)
  Voyetra Technologies
  5 Odell Plaza
  Yonkers, NY 10701-1406
  (914) 966-0600

Wave Editor (Windows; see Chapter 10)
  Starlite Software
  Distributed by:
  Advanced Support Group
  11900 Grant Pl.
  Des Peres, MO 63131
  Orders: (800) 767-9611

INDEX

speech *(cont.)*
  recognition. voice recognition
  sampling frequencies for, 16, 40
  unvoiced sounds, 48
  viewing, 49-51
  voiced sounds, 48
sustain, 79
synthesizer basics, 70-71

T
timbre, 5, 78
tone, 5
tremolo, 12, 84

V
VDEMO, 51-54
vibrato, 12, 68-69, 84
.VOC files
  defined, 24, 149
  making .WAV files from, 132
  players for, 24-30, 118
voice recognition
  suppliers of software for, 159-160
  trainable system, 137-139
  types of, 51
  under Windows, 137-139
  voice command game, 51-54
  voice response systems, 46
volume, 5

W
Walsh, Craig, 9
.WAV files
  3-D sound, 62-64

.WAV files *(cont.)*
  converting .VOC files to, 132
  editors for
    DOS, 24-30
    Windows, 135-137
  explained, 150
  player for, 131-132
Wave Editor, 135-137, 154
Wave for Windows, displayed
  waveforms using, 11-13
waveforms
  analysis of, 9-11
  viewing
    under DOS, 6-9, 35-38
    under Windows, 135-137
Weiner, Kevin
  bio, vi
  email address, vi
Whoop It Up!, 132-134
Windows
  attaching sounds to events or
    programs, 132-134
  drivers, 131
  interface with sound devices,
    129-131
  Media Control Interface, 131
  Media Player program,
    131-132
  voice recognition under,
    137-139
Word Scope, 49-51
WSCOPE, 49-51

Y
Young, Jim (u4ia), 107

167

Books have a substantial influence on the destruction of the forests of the Earth. For example, it takes 17 trees to produce one ton of paper. A first printing of 30,000 copies of a typical 480 page book consumes 108,000 pounds of paper which will require 918 trees!

Waite Group Press™ is against the clear-cutting of forests and supports reforestation of the Pacific Northwest of the United States and Canada, where most of this paper comes from. As a publisher with several hundred thousand books sold each year, we feel an obligation to give back to the planet. We will therefore support and contribute a percentage of our proceeds to organizations which seek to preserve the forests of planet Earth.

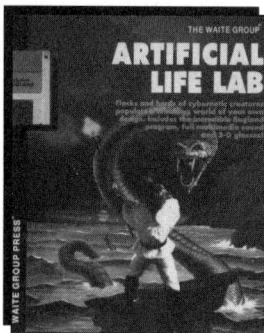

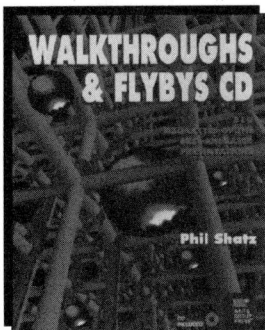

SOFTWARE LICENSE AGREEMENT

SATISFACTION REPORT CARD

Please fill out this card if you wish to know of future updates to *Sound Effects Playhouse*, or to receive our catalog.

WAITE GROUP PRESS™

Company Name: _____

Division/Department: _____ Mail Stop: _____

Last Name: _____ First Name: _____ Middle Initial: _____

Street Address: _____

City: _____ State: _____ Zip: _____

Daytime telephone: (___) _____

Date product was acquired: Month ____ Day ____ Year ____ Your Occupation: _____

Overall, how would you rate *Sound Effects Playhouse?*
- ☐ Excellent
- ☐ Very Good
- ☐ Good
- ☐ Fair
- ☐ Below Average
- ☐ Poor

What did you like MOST about this book? _____
_____

What did you like LEAST about this book? _____
_____
_____

Please describe any problems you may have encountered with installing or using the disk: _____
_____

How did you use this book (problem-solver, tutorial, reference...)?
_____

What is your level of computer expertise?
- ☐ New
- ☐ Dabbler
- ☐ Hacker
- ☐ Power User
- ☐ Programmer
- ☐ Experienced Professional

What computer applications do you use most? _____
_____

Please describe your computer hardware:
Computer _____ Hard disk _____
5.25" disk drives _____ 3.5" disk drives _____
Video card _____ Monitor _____
Printer _____ Peripherals _____
Sound Board _____ CD ROM _____

Where did you buy this book?
- ☐ Bookstore (name): _____
- ☐ Discount store (name): _____
- ☐ Computer store (name): _____
- ☐ Catalog (name): _____
- ☐ Direct from WGP   ☐ Other _____

What price did you pay for this book? _____

What influenced your purchase of this book?
- ☐ Recommendation
- ☐ Magazine review
- ☐ Mailing
- ☐ Reputation of Waite Group Press
- ☐ Advertisement
- ☐ Store display
- ☐ Book's format
- ☐ Other

How many computer books do you buy each year? _____

How many other Waite Group books do you own? _____

What is your favorite Waite Group book? _____
_____

Is there any program or subject you would like to see Waite Group Press cover in a similar approach? _____
_____
_____

Additional comments? _____
_____
_____

☐ **Check here for a free Waite Group catalog**

Sound Effects Playhouse

Waite Group Press, Inc.
Attention: *Sound Effects Playhouse*
200 Tamal Plaza
Corte Madera, CA 94925

FOLD HERE